PEDALING THE SACRIFICE ZONE

THE SEVENTH GENERATION
Survival, Sustainability, Sustenance in a New Nature
M. Jimmie Killingsworth, Series Editor

A WARDLAW BOOK

PEDALING THE SACRIFICE ZONE

Teaching, Writing, & Living above the Marcellus Shale

JIMMY GUIGNARD

Photographs by Steven Rubin, Maps by Andy Shears

Foreword by M. Jimmie Killingsworth

TEXAS A&M UNIVERSITY PRESS • COLLEGE STATION, TEXAS

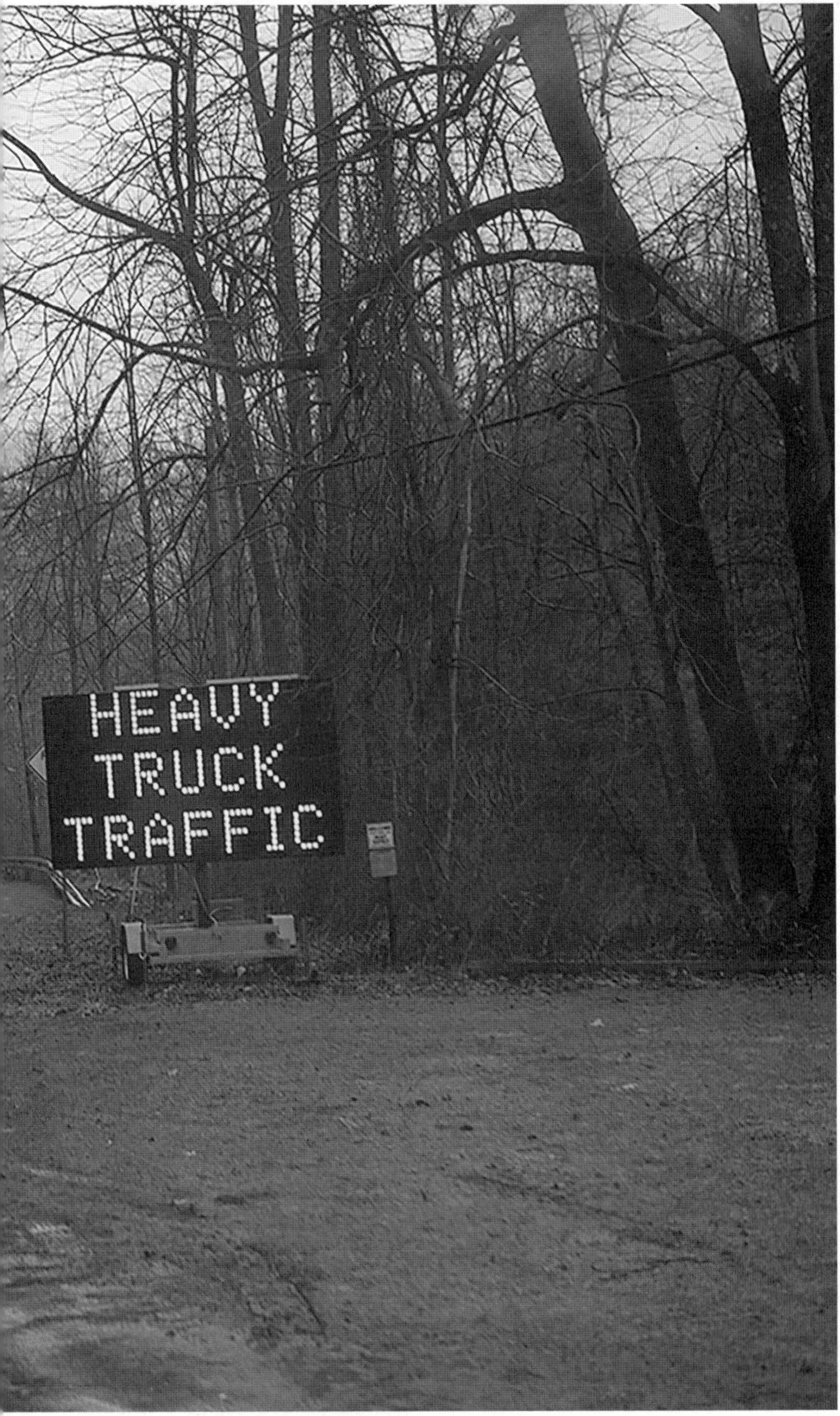
HEAVY
TRUCK
TRAFFIC

This paper meets the requirements of
ANSI/NISO Z39.48-1992
(Permanence of Paper).
Binding materials have been
chosen for durability.
Manufactured in the United States of America

LIBRARY OF CONGRESS CATALOGING-IN-PUBLICATION DATA

Guignard, James, author.
    Pedaling the sacrifice zone: teaching, writing, and living above the Marcellus
Shale / Jimmy Guignard; photographs by Steven Rubin; maps by Andy Shears;
foreword by M. Jimmie Killingsworth. — First edition.
            pages cm — (Seventh generation: survival, sustainability, sustenance in
a new nature)
    Includes bibliographical references and index.
    ISBN 978-1-62349-351-6 (pbk.: alk. paper) —
    ISBN 978-1-62349-352-3 (ebook)
    1. Guignard, James. 2. Rhetoricians—Pennsylvania—Tioga County—
Biography. 3. Conservationists—Pennsylvania—Tioga County—Biography.
4. Tioga County (Pa.)—Environmental conditions. 5. Marcellus Shale—
Environmental conditions. 6. Shale gas industry—Environmental aspects—
Pennsylvania. 7. Ecocriticism. I. Killingsworth, M. Jimmie, writer of
preface. II. Title. III. Series: Seventh generation (Series)
    PE64.G85A3 2015
    818'.603—dc23
                        2015012198

Cover photo and photo on series page by Lilace Mellin Guignard.

Contents

Foreword

✳ The idea of starting a new series at Texas A&M University Press on survival, sustainability, and sustenance was still a dream with a good chance of coming into reality when I first met James Guignard. I was giving a talk about nature writing for an undergraduate conference at Susquehanna University, to which Professor Guignard had brought a group of his students from Mansfield. Jimmy recognized in my accent a fellow Carolinian and told me a little about his adjustment to life in Pennsylvania after graduate study in Reno. We talked about writing and place. (As our fellow series author Sid Dobrin has pithily said, "Writing takes place.")

Over the next weeks, we started up an email correspondence. I read his blog about living, bicycling, and teaching over the Marcellus shale, the fracking of which was turning the rural countryside around Mansfield into a new world—more profitable for some, more dangerous and disturbing for others, but different for everyone. The image of Jimmy on his bike, or in the classroom, or in his old house with his young family, puzzling over what was happening to the place around him, proved irresistible to me. I told him about the series and urged him to submit a proposal. He bought into the dream. He wrote the book. The reality exceeded the dream.

I cannot imagine a better contribution to the series, now called Seventh Generation: The Survival, Sustainability, Sustenance in a New Nature, than this book. It questions the sustainability of ramped-up gas production in the rural countryside resulting from the high demand for US-produced gas and oil to meet the ever-increasing energy needs of the nation. It introduces a personal narrative that ponders the survival of a pastoral life in the country in places that have become sacrifice zones, dedicated to satisfying the same demands for cheap and somewhat cleaner fuel. And it offers a meditation on sustenance—literally in its treatment of how local water is affected by industry and the challenges of those committed to the local food movement and figuratively in facing the question of what sustains us—what kind of work, what kind of home, what kind of physical activity, what kind of connections with people and nature. As a highly original book, it perfectly fulfills the goal of the series to engage environmental topics with the spirit of expertise and research but in language that narrates rather than lectures (or preaches) and that aspires to reach a broadly educated audience.

The unique perspective that Jimmy brings results from a combination of elements. Above all, there's the bicycling. His rides through the Pennsylvania hills and valleys over the past few years tie the whole together. These episodes merge with the style and viewpoint more often associated with the best nature writing. He combines the action of high-speed, long-distance riding with the close observation and delight in discovering along the way the presence of scarlet tanagers, pileated woodpeckers, wild turkeys, and the occasional bobcat with young. He gives a detailed record of the changes wrought by the extraction of natural gas from this land, a record compiled from daily observations of a man who over the past eight years has traversed the byways of Tioga County at the rate of 3,000 miles a year. The free-wheeling bicycle enthusiast with his fondness for family life, good friends, bourbon, and craft-brewed beer somehow melds seamlessly with the concerned citizen, devoted teacher, rhetorical scholar, and increasingly committed activist who learns in the course of the story to process chickens and turkeys and also finds his way into local environmental politics. Finally, there's the sheer volume of information—

factual, anecdotal, and analytical—that the author brings from his personal research on the controversy. From reading Jimmy's work, I've learned a great deal about the effects of fracking and natural gas extraction and the effects on rural lands. And I never felt the strong need to filter the information because this book works so hard to account for the author's own biases and shifting viewpoints and to question the agendas of others, whether they are industry reps, local folks, academic scientists, or hard-line environmentalists.

Ultimately, *Pedaling the Sacrifice Zone* is a rare example of rhetorical analysis in action, performing the hard work of constantly filtering and re-filtering information, not in the safely enclosed space of the think tank or academic journal but in a personal narrative set in a place that really matters to the author. It is a rich reading experience that promises to alter the way we see the world. In the place of mechanical objectivity, it urges honesty. And instead of ideological stridency, it offers one man's testimony, remarkably told.

M. Jimmie Killingsworth
Series Editor

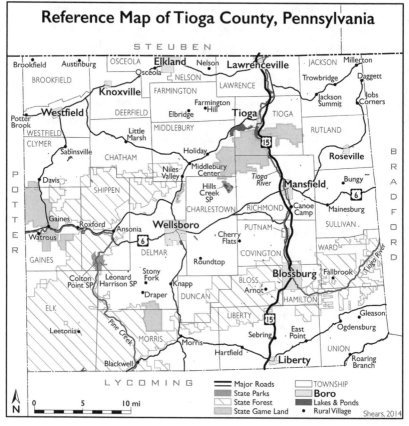

Reference Map of Tioga County, Pennsylvania

Map by Andy Shears

Preface

⌗   *Pedaling the Sacrifice Zone* tells the story of me and my family moving to a blank space on a map and trying to turn the space into a place. After we'd lived here a while and were putting down roots, along came the natural gas industry. It tried to turn our place back into a blank space. The university where I teach participated in this boom-and-bust cycle in surprising ways as well. All of this caught us off guard and threw us into a frenzy of choices about whether to stay or go, to live in town or move to the country, to put down more roots or pull them up. I was drawn into the daily struggle of watching a place I was falling in love with get used like an old bike rag. *Pedaling the Sacrifice Zone* drills into my struggle to understand how industry and rhetoric shape the way I experience the rural place my wife and I chose to settle in as it transforms into an industrial sacrifice zone.

Warning: I was a redneck before I was an academic and don't much enjoy that impersonal academic voice. So imagine I'm telling you this story outside around a fire, beer or bourbon (or both) in hand. Grab that chair, and get comfortable. I'll get some more wood.

Acknowledgments

✳   I had a lot of help with this book, so I owe the following people thanks: Bruce Barton, Mike and Chris Chester, Ada Mae Compton, Dave Darby, Jen Demchak, John Derry, Russ Dodson, Melissa Goldthwaite, Billy Guignard, LuAnn Guignard, Sam Guignard, Terri Guignard, Hannah Killian, Chris Kopf, Ed Kozaczka, Sarafina Milatello, Tom and Madalene Murphy, Bob Myers, Ben Nevin, Lisa Parker, Lynn Pifer, Terre Ryan, Kristin Sanner, Judith Sornberger, David Stinebeck, Anne Styborski, Louise Sullivan-Blum, John Ulrich, Anna Ward, Jim Weaver, Todd Webster, Paul and Joyce Wendel, and Thad and Nikki York. Note that this book contains information throughout from a chapter I contributed in 2013: "A Certain Uncertainty: Drilling Into the Rhetoric of the Marcellus Shale Natural Gas Development," in Peter N. Goggin (Ed.), *Environmental Rhetoric and Ecologies of Place,* pp. 15–27 (New York: Routledge, 2013).

Thanks to Steven Rubin for providing his stunning photos, and thanks to Andy Shears for making the kick-ass maps. Thanks to Mansfield University for providing me with a sabbatical in fall 2013. A huge thanks to Martin and Heather Kohout and their outstanding Madroño Ranch Writer's Residency, which provided me with twelve days of uninterrupted writing among the bison, wild turkeys, and wild pigs. Thanks to Jimmie Killingsworth for seeing the possibilities in this book and to Shannon Davies for having patience with me.

Thanks to the other three-quarters of the Four Horses' Asses of the Apocalypse: Tom Oswald, Francis Craig, and Dan Styborski. And I have to thank the Old Man, Eric Franck. He made me appreciate Tioga County in new ways. All four suffered me talking through ideas for many miles of pedaling. As if the pedaling wasn't tough enough.

As I wrote, I had three dedicated readers who gave unflinching feedback: Julia Kasdorf, Sheila Kasperek, and Steve Tchudi. This book is better because of you.

Finally, I have to thank my wife Lilace (whose feedback made me flinch—in a good way) and my kids, Gabe and Gloria, for putting up with my crap over the past few years. I'm lucky to have y'all.

PEDALING THE SACRIFICE ZONE

1 Not NIMBYs

⌗   "I've found another house for us to look at," my wife said to me one Friday in April 2009. I had finished teaching for the week, and we were standing in our tiny kitchen, having found a lull during a hectic time of the semester at Mansfield University (MU). We lived in Tioga County in northcentral Pennsylvania, one of the busiest counties during the Marcellus shale natural gas boom. I could hear trucks rattling by on Route 6 about 100 yards behind our house as anger whooshed through my belly like a flared well. I didn't want to move. I was scared of the industry rolling by on Route 6. I looked down. She rushed on. "It's on top of Pickle Hill, it has a big yard, and it's on unleased land." *Here we go again*, I thought, jaw clenching.

"I don't think we should move," I said. "It's the wrong time. If the gas industry screws up our water, we're fucked." I stared at our gas stove, the black and silver finish blurring as I fought to control my temper. Her obsession with moving out of town made me mad, and we had a version of this conversation often over several months. I recited my next line in our script: "We should wait and see what happens with the industry. I don't want to spend $300,000 on a house and lose it all. That's what will happen if they fuck up our water. We'll have nothing."

"No, it won't," Lilace shot back. She had more confidence than me in our ability to make the industry accountable for any problems it caused us. Lilace knew my one hard home-buying rule was that the house had to sit on unleased land, one she agreed with. Even so, I wasn't convinced that my English professor salary and her part-timer pay could mount a serious challenge to the likes of Royal Dutch Shell, should they trash our property or, worse, wreck our health. Our brains were our biggest assets, and I wasn't sure that was enough. I thought buying a house in the country in the middle of the Marcellus shale gas rush was about the stupidest thing I could imagine doing. I could imagine drill rigs sprouting from our back-yard, while water trucks like the ones outside made hundreds of trips past our front yard, blanketing our country retreat with dust, noise, and diesel exhaust. So much for using our assets.

I was baffled by Lilace's attitude toward the industry's presence and couldn't wrap my head around her willingness to move into what amounted to an industrial zone. This was the woman who had read Rachel Carson's *Silent Spring* and Sandra Steingraber's *Living Downstream* and *Having Faith*. She thought carefully about how the environment affects children. She breastfed our son until he was two and a half, watched food choices carefully, limited time in front of the tube, ensured that the kids got lots of sleep—all those things that great moms do. She pointed out, accurately, that environmentalists often portray the worst or pick the most extreme examples when arguing for a particular view on gas development. *But, but, Lilace*, I thought, *your mom had cancer. Cancer!* Though, truthfully, her mom's cancer had nothing to do with the gas indus-try. In my fear of losing everything, I simply couldn't see why she wasn't more concerned about the possibility of our water being ruined or the kids huffing benzene. Or how she could be so sure that we could fight it. I imagined the worst, and I suspected that all the glowing recommendations of the industry were not as bright as the industry made them out to be. I knew Lilace knew this too. As she pointed out, rightly, "We won't escape the industry in town!" At times, my anger with Lilace bubbled up as good, old-fashioned patriarchy: *I bring home the damn cash, woman! We're not moving!* At least I was smart enough not to say this out loud.

Lilace was motivated by concerns other than fear of the gas industry, namely that our kids needed a bigger yard to run wild and ride bikes in, and we needed to trade the sound of drunken college kids for owls and coyotes. She cared about the effects of the industry, but she cared more about writing, gardening, raising chickens, and our kids running free—a lifestyle more suited to our sensibilities. She needed nature to live and respite from being woken at night by drunk college students. She also found that looking out her study at houses and power lines smothered her creativity. I understood her perspective—I prefer birds and trees to houses and power lines—and I loved the idea of our kids playing war and cowboys and Indians like I did when I was a kid. But I have a tendency to endure, to hunker down, and to make changes only when they promise greater things, like moving to Nevada for grad school and easy access to Sierra Nevada rock climbing. Or marrying the woman I now argued with. Most of the time, I'd rather be riding my bike than doing the heavy lifting (physical or mental) that change requires. I couldn't see those "greater things" for the dust kicked up by the gas trucks. I would no longer be able to walk to work, the bar, or the bike shop. I'd have a bigger yard, but that meant mowing. I hate mowing. Most pressing, I had uncertainty hanging over my head in the form of a band of natural gas–laden shale 5,000 feet underground.

As we argued and looked at houses over the months, hundreds of sand, water, and dump trucks rumbled through town daily, and white pickups with out-of-state plates jammed the parking spaces on Main Street. I didn't want to make this move, this *change*, because I feared the change rumbling through our town and county could be carrying our health and security to a landfill or an open wastewater pit. I didn't want us to become "Residual Waste," words on the magnetic signs stuck to dump trucks hauling nonhazardous and "near hazardous" waste for the industry ("What Is Residual Waste" 2015). Where Lilace saw escape, I saw risk. I thought I had a pretty tight case.

I stomped off to my office upstairs to stare at the ornamental crabapple outside the window where cedar waxwings stopped in May. If only Lilace was as quiet and satisfied as those mysterious gray birds, damn it! We looked at the house on Pickle Hill and decided to put in an offer, mostly because of its location (close to campus and friends), the awesome great room upstairs, and the expansive views of a valley. Since we couldn't swing two house payments a month, our offer depended on us selling our house. In the end, we missed out on the Pickle Hill house because ours didn't sell in time.

Now there's a well pad across the road from that house.

—◇—

I am a professor of English at Mansfield University in Mansfield, Pennsylvania. My specialty is composition and rhetoric, which means I teach students to write and to analyze how texts— written, spoken, and visual—attempt to make us think in certain ways or to adopt certain attitudes. My job requires that I take a disinterested view of multiple perspectives and hard evidence to reach the most informed, thoughtful ideas or conclusions possible at a given time. My field of rhetoric, however, recognizes that these are ideals to strive for and that any time we use language, the words or images we use have some sort of bias or slant built in that inclines people toward whatever outcome the speaker or writer desires. Everyone practices rhetoric to some extent, even my son at three years old. My mom tells the story of riding with him through Charlotte, North Carolina, when he spied the Golden Arches. Gabe said, "My mama won't take me to McDonald's, but my daddy's mama sure can." I love this story and share it with my classes. I tell students, "Notice that he didn't say 'daddy' but 'mama,' pitting female against female, and he recognized that my wife's and my rules for eating were likely to be bent with Grandma, something he'd experienced before. The kid understood his audience." To this day, I can imagine my mom swerving across several lanes of South Boulevard traffic hell-bent to buy her grandson some French fries.

One important practice in my field—rhetoric—is that we try to "prove opposites." We try on arguments from opposing views in order to reach the most satisfactory conclusion for all interested parties. The practice of "proving opposites" expects us to get inside the heads of the people we are trying to persuade, whether we agree with them or not, so we understand where others are coming from and shape our messages accordingly. This requires us to suspend judgment, a difficult thing to do, though I've always been slow to judge (except about beer, bikes, and barbecue), so taking this perspective suits me well.

I teach this process of proving opposites to my students, pushing them to recognize that whatever they bring to a given argument or situation is crucial to their understanding of it, and I push them to see beyond their first impressions. I bring my background as college professor, father, husband, cyclist, construction worker, environmentalist, truck driver's son, and Southerner, among other things, to bear on my understanding of natural gas, and I try to show my students how these and other facets of my identity affect the way I understand the industry and the world encompassing it. I draw on my experiences with those dimensions (and others) of my identity as I seek out ways to create the life I want for me and my family. I value some aspects of my identity more than others, but all of them contribute to my understanding of how I see the world and where I want it to go. My wife's and my arguments about whether we should move out of town created a clash between my professional identity and my identity as a father, husband, and citizen of Tioga County. The disinterested researcher in me found it difficult to stay disinterested when I read stories about Dimock, Pennsylvania, a place where Cabot Oil and Gas Corporation polluted sixteen families' wells. It also made it difficult for me to try on my wife's perspective and really understand where she was coming from. Hers was a different "opposite," concerned with different issues. Her position was not the industry's, but I saw it that way at the time, unfairly so. In my studies of environmental issues, I read about industrial impacts on the environment and saw the impacts in pictures and films. I learned how the industries fought to control the message in order to run roughshod over the communities, often in the name of jobs or security or patriotism. When it came to Lilace, I wasn't practicing what I preached about proving opposites.

As Lilace and I fought over whether to move, I watched the trucks rumble by, sometimes waiting for several minutes to cross Route 6 on my walk to work—a road my kids would have to cross if they ever walked to school alone. On my bike rides, I saw the well pads carved out of the farmland, sprouting drill rigs my wife described as the middle finger of progress. I read voraciously about natural gas, learning quickly that the technology of high-volume slickwater hydraulic fracturing was impressive and had a track record of about a decade, which meant little science to support or deny its safety. I attended meetings put on by the industry and universities and talked with everyone I could about their experiences with natural gas development. Living in the midst of a natural gas boom and the web of words that support it has changed my understanding of how language works, akin to the way shifting from riding a 35-pound steel Wal-Mart bike to a 17-pound carbon fiber Specialized road bike changes the way a person rides.

—◦—

The story has been (and is still being) told about the physical changes to the communities and the landscape brought about by the Marcellus shale boom. Like all stories, there are competing versions. My story is different. I don't have a success story of becoming a shaleionaire or a horror story of burning faucets (though I've heard plenty of both). My story tells of a teacher, writer, husband, and father trying to make the right decisions and live a good life where the gas industry spreads in all directions and threatens to change what I love about this place—a place where the information needed to make good decisions seems as difficult to access as the natural gas trapped in the shale several thousand feet below us. I tell the story of how the rhetoric of industry, politicians, and locals combined to create a confusing web of words that reshaped my understanding of place and teaching and called into question my belief in the power of rhetoric, a realization that rocks me to the core. Put another way, this book is rhetorical analysis made personal. If language can't change minds, can't persuade people to care about more than padding a bank account, how will we ever take care of ourselves and the land we live on?

—◦—

When Lilace and I started arguing about moving to the country in 2008, we'd lived in Tioga County for about four years, and we were realizing how the gas industry was going to change everything. Because my wife is the planner—I'm usually thinking about my next beer or bike ride—she had scoured the Internet realty sites for houses soon after I accepted the job at Mansfield University, and she planned a trip to Mansfield for us to look at houses soon after my dissertation advisor hooded me at the University of Nevada, Reno. In May 2005, we drove into Mansfield and stayed with Rob and Cindy at their B&B, the same place I stayed during my on-campus job interview, while we looked at houses in and out of town. We settled on a house in town, a huge, gorgeous Victorian built in the 1870s with eight-foot ceilings, chestnut molding, huge bedrooms, tiny bathrooms, a tiny kitchen, a tiny yard, and a shared driveway that was about a five-minute walk from my office. The house was twice as big as our house in Reno, half the price, and three times as cold in winter. It was definitely "of its time," though we updated the house with a gas fireplace, stainless steel refrigerator, pellet stove, and insulation. The energy contractor who insulated the walls with shredded paper and patched holes with expanding foam informed us that the entire house was sheathed in 2×6s, a holdover from when timber was the natural resource du jour. That 2×6s were used where contractors now use plywood or oriented strand board boggles this former construction worker's mind.

Over time we settled into the slow-paced rural college town where the single stoplight began blinking yellow at 11:00 p.m. Not that I was often up to see it. I loved the snail's pace, the near desolation in summer (the students were gone!), the lazy evenings in the backyard with burgers and beer. Though I knew I was privileged, the pangs I felt at people struggling to find a living wage paled in comparison to the satisfaction I felt at living a small, quiet life where I may see two people, and I know both of them, on my five-minute walk to the coffee shop. Our son attended the local nursery school, played soccer and baseball, and made friends. Lilace got involved in St. James Episcopal Church, formed a writer's group, and, with two close friends, founded the Mansfield Grower's Market, now in its fifth year. Our daughter, born in February 2007 during a subzero cold spell, grew out of diapers and breastfeeding. I taught classes, worked toward tenure and promotion, and rode bikes about 100 miles a week with a small crew of local diehards. I was quickly smitten by the country roads and the endless rolling hills covered in trees.

Our son was growing more mobile, and his backyard adventures grew to include castles, forts, and massive army or superhero battles. Lilace recognized that the six-foot wooden fence we built around the backyard confined him, though she liked the fact that it kept him safe. We saw how happy he was running wild with his friends out in Bungy or up on Reese Hill. The guy's got a big imagination, and our small yard hemmed it in. Lilace was feeling confined too—looking out the windows at power lines and houses fenced in her imagination. Plus, we didn't need 3,100 square feet of house. Even so, when Lilace suggested we downsize the house and increase the land, I resisted. The gas industry had been rumbling by for a few months and showed no signs of slowing down. I figured we could take Gabe out to the state game lands or to friends' houses to let him exercise that imagination. I wanted my son and daughter to grow up in the woods like I did, but based on what I was learning about the gas industry, I was willing to let them suck it up in a tiny yard, no matter how bored they got. Lilace persisted, and we began looking at houses in 2008. For me, as the industry revved up, our idyll idled down.

As I write this in 2014, over 4,000 natural gas wells have been drilled in Pennsylvania into the Marcellus shale ("Marcellus Shale—Appalachian Basin" n.d.). Before the dust settles, as many as 100,000 wells may be drilled on 20,000 well pads.[1] From the activity I saw on my bike rides and walks, there was gas everywhere. In 2008, when we started looking at houses, it looked like the United States needed *all* of the gas *right now*. White pick-ups with Texas and Oklahoma plates dotted the roads. Sand trucks, tanker trucks, and dump trucks plastered with the words "Residual Waste" rumbled through town. Three-quarter-ton flat-bed duallies hauled assorted parts, welders, and job boxes up and down our street, carrying gas workers to rented houses to sleep off twelve-hour shifts. Our big Victorian house sat over one of the thickest sections of Marcellus shale—400 feet thick. Signs of the industry were everywhere.

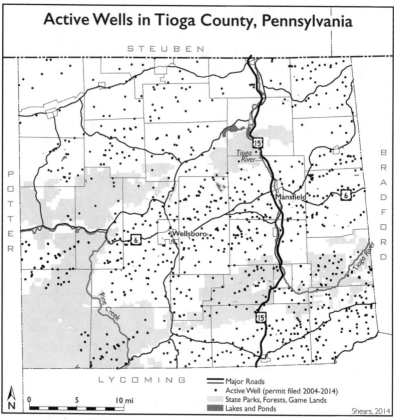

Active Wells in Tioga County, Pennsylvania

STEUBEN

POTTER

BRADFORD

Tioga River

Mansfield

Wellsboro

Pine Creek

Tioga River

LYCOMING

Major Roads
• Active Well (permit filed 2004-2014)
State Parks, Forests, Game Lands
Lakes and Ponds

Shears, 2014

N
0   5   10 mi

Map by Andy Shears

The influx of the industry reminded me of a military invasion, merging in my mind with images from war movies like *Patton*, *Apocalypse Now*, *The Dirty Dozen*, and *Saving Private Ryan*. In one scene, as Francis and I rode our road bikes around the Five Hills loop between Mansfield and Wellsboro, a blue helicopter trailing a large orange basket swooped around the hills a few hundred feet off the ground. As we rode, we watched the helicopter flying back and forth across Cherry Flats Road, like the choppers swooping over the hamlet in the beach scene in *Apocalypse Now*. The helicopter was seismic testing for gas deposits. I expected "Flight of the Valkyries" any second.

Cut to Scene II. My daughter and I walked out of Night and Day Coffee Café on the corner of Route 6 and Old Highway 15 and turned east on 6 toward the university. We were 10 feet away from the pavement, and triaxle trucks roared by nonstop, creaking and rattling under the weight of residual waste and frack water, spitter valves bleeding pressure and moisture from the brake systems. She covered her ears and gritted her teeth. Scene III: On my way to teach one day, I walked in Night and Day for an Americano. I asked Jess, the owner, where all the damn trucks were coming from. She laughed and told me that customers had counted as many as a hundred trucks passing outside the window in an hour.

In the final scene, a group of cyclists sat around a table covered with pitchers of beer and bowls of peanuts on the back patio of Changos Cantina on Wednesday night. Known as Man Night,[2] the group laughed over the racing shenanigans that occurred during that night's 35-mile ride. Burly guys sporting deep tans and bright orange and yellow safety shirts drank beer and shot pool nearby. There was a crowd at the bar, more burly florescent dudes, and it took a while to buy a pitcher of Yuengling. We leaned in close to hear each other over the noise, though we were amped from a hard ride and loud too. The gas guys bothered us only when they smoked. Francis told them, "Hey, you can't smoke out here." Apologizing, they extinguished their cigarettes.

I lived scenes like these while Lilace and I argued about buying in the country. She lived similar scenes, but more often hers involved sitting in the house and trying to grow a garden while students smashed her squash in the street. Hardly a satisfying home life. We educated ourselves about the industry. I read articles from professors at Penn State and Cornell's Cooperative Exchange. I attended meetings, both industry and academic. I followed what our local and state politicians said about the development of shale. I learned about royalties and severance taxes and the Safe Drinking Water Act. I read the local paper and the Sierra Club's and National Resources Defense Council's missives. And I kept getting angrier at what appeared to me to be an industry catching all the breaks as it crowded the roads and the restaurants and carved well pads and pipeline right-of-ways out of Tioga County's fields and forests.

—◦—

My first close encounter with the gas industry came at an informational meeting on June 4, 2009, hosted by the Marcellus Shale Committee (now the Marcellus Shale Coalition [MSC]), the main industry (read: lobbying) group in Pennsylvania. I drove to the Wellsboro High School auditorium because I wanted to hear industry reps firsthand and see the audience's reaction (you know, that whole "informed citizen" thing). I settled in my seat with around 125 others, clustered in groups of twos and threes. Most wore sweatshirts, Carhartts, and baseball caps. I wore Patagonia fleece and a knit cap. The presenters sat at a table to the right of the stage while a projector showed a computer-generated cutaway view of a gas well on a huge screen to the left. People talked quietly among themselves. I opened my journal and prepared to take notes, curious about what I'd learn about the industry and the public's reaction to it.

Louis D'Amico of the MSC, two local gas executives, and two public relations employees represented the industry. County Commissioner Erick Coolidge introduced the group, saying, "Many states don't have the choice we have," before taking a seat in the audience.[3] D'Amico stood up, and we were treated to a polished and informative presentation about drilling for natural gas in the

Marcellus shale, including a short, computer-generated video that illustrated high-volume slickwater hydraulic fracturing clearly. It was an impressive presentation that raised all sorts of questions for me, mostly because it sounded too good to be true.

One issue that bothered me from the outset about drilling for natural gas concerned water use. The industry knows people are concerned, and it makes water use sound as innocuous as possible. The technology of slickwater hydraulic fracturing required to free the gas from the shale requires an enormous amount of water per well, somewhere between one and five million gallons. The process is known as "fracking."[4] Industry representatives made the amounts sound risk-free. D'Amico stated that the natural gas industry used the equivalent of 1 percent of the entire daily amount of water used in the state of Pennsylvania and less water in a day than is required for Pennsylvania's golf courses. According to a 2000 US Geological Survey study, Pennsylvania used five billion to ten billion gallons of water per day. That means the natural gas industry is adding fifty million to one hundred million gallons of water to Pennsylvania's existing water requirements. D'Amico downplayed the substantial burden on local and other water sources, especially the long-range implications. Once water is used for fracking, it is essentially taken out of an ecosystem, unlike water sprayed on golf courses. Water is becoming a scarcer resource each year, yet the gas industry's way of presenting the information focuses the public's attention on smaller numbers, not larger ones. As my friend, geology professor Chris Kopf, told me, "The problem here is that all the water goes somewhere else. It looks like we have a lot, but we really don't."

The industry portrayed the composition of frack water in favorable terms as well. Frack water is a blend of water, sand, and chemicals that is pumped into a drilled well and blasted into the shale. Forced into the shale, the mixture drains back into the well bore, leaving "proppants" consisting of sand or ceramic particles in the fractures to hold them open and allow gas to flow into the drill bore. D'Amico explained that frack water is composed of 90 percent water, 9.95 percent sand, and .05 percent chemicals. The small percentage of chemicals sounds safe, the equivalent of a drop of Coors Light in your microbrew, but the fact that each well requires somewhere between one million and five million gallons of water suggests a large amount of chemicals are pumped into the ground. Based on the industry's percentages, that means somewhere in the range of 50,000 to 250,000 gallons of chemicals are used per well. That's a lot of Coors Light. Because of what I had been reading elsewhere, I noticed that D'Amico forgot to mention that the drillers can only pump out around 60 percent of the frack water, which means 40 percent of it stays in the ground. Nor did he mention the risk of spills, an "oversight" that I found damning once I learned that Pennsylvania had been experiencing spills and polluted water wells.[5]

Not only does the industry try to downplay the amounts of chemicals used; it also portrays the chemicals as harmless. The chemicals used in fracking are mixed in proprietary formulas, and, at the time, the people living here did not know what chemicals were being pumped into the ground at any given drill site. But the gas industry handles this point of contention deftly by pointing out that many of the chemicals are found in most households. Addressing concerns about the secretive nature of the frack fluid, D'Amico stated, "Everyone knows what is in the fluid," before explaining that the proprietary knowledge stems from the *ratios* of the chemicals in the mix. He then claimed that the chemicals can be found in "consumer goods and cosmetics." D'Amico's characterization of the chemicals suggests that the entire process of fracking is harmless, equating thousands of gallons of chemicals mixed with sand and water with items we keep in our sheds and medicine cabinets. As I listened to D'Amico, I realized that the strategy used by the industry to shape public perception of the chemicals compromised the public's ability to assess the risks.[6] I had to go elsewhere to learn that some of the chemicals found in frack water include a liner gel delivery system consisting mostly of diesel fuel,[7] a known carcinogen; a crosslinker consisting of boric acid, ethylene glycol, and monoethanolamine, a possible carcinogen that may cause birth defects; and a foaming agent consisting of isopropanol, salt of alkyl amines, and diethanolamine, known carcinogens. According to the Environmental Protection Agency, frack fluid contains as many as sixteen components, each of which consists of one or more chemicals. The ecological impact of many of the chemicals is unknown.

At the time, I wondered whether the characterization of the contents of the fracking chemicals was honest. Yes, these chemicals may appear in consumer goods and cosmetics. But I don't whip out my gallon of muriatic acid[8] and knock back a couple of shots on Friday night. Hell, Timothy McVeigh used consumer goods to make a bomb.

This meeting represented the nature of much of the information in Tioga County at the time, and it serves as a good example of how messages are shaped to push people to think in certain ways. The meeting made gas development sound great, and it set a direction for public discourse that clashed with my training as an academic and my beliefs as a citizen. There was nothing disinterested about this meeting.[9] The structure of the meeting suggested that the gas industry executives knew if they controlled the message, they controlled the county's image of the industry. The format set the industry reps up as experts and enabled them to provide information in terms favorable to their interests. That's a problem for a public struggling to understand, and it bugged the hell out of me. This is an especially powerful practice in an economically depressed area where less than 18 percent of the population has a postsecondary degree and many struggle to keep family farms solvent. When people who live here think of natural gas, they often think "money," and understandably so. When the gas industry people presented information, they used the public's reaction to help them shape, to the industry's advantage, the way people view drilling. I'm trained to see complexity, and while it showed the complexity of the gas drilling process itself, the meeting provided little in the way of addressing complex social and environmental concerns. Needless to say, the Wellsboro meeting did not increase my confidence in our decision to buy a house out of town.

—◦—

The claims I heard in the high school auditorium were echoed in many conversations I had with other people. The claims also appeared in Pennsylvania newspapers. Ads for such meetings appeared in the local newspaper, and though I always looked for signs of neutrality, I rarely found them in Pennsylvania. The state seemed to throw its weight behind the industry, which was not surprising, given the Commonwealth's history with extractive industries.[10] Gas industry officials presented themselves as the "experts," and rightfully so when it came to gas extraction. But other issues, like social and environmental costs that fell outside their expertise, were glossed over or ignored. There was no way to debate the issue either. Rhetoric expects me to consider an issue from multiple perspectives, but I was only getting one perspective—the industry's. The lack of a disinterested voice on the Wellsboro panel suggested that concerns that might challenge the industry's perspective were not worth pursuing. This results in what, speaking about the media, Nancy Welch calls a "problem of *ethos* [because such arrangements] predispose us to define very narrowly what constitutes an authoritative appeal" (2008, 135). Authority was given only to the industry, a group with a vested interest in making people see things their way (in other words: public relations). D'Amico was a lobbyist for the gas industry. Questions about environmental impacts, taxes, and the like were relegated to the Q&A portion of the meeting, if they were raised at all. In fact, most questions for the panelists revolved around why East Resources was trying to lower landowners' lease offers, which I knew nothing about until the meeting and which I found disconcerting. If the development of natural gas as a resource was such an economic boon, why was East trying to change its leases?

Questions about why East Resources was trying to renegotiate its leases dominated the first part of Q&A, perhaps understandably—people had money at stake—but I thought about issues like water use and pollution and whether the industry would pay its fair share for being here. During a lull, I asked the panel to explain why the industry should not pay a severance tax (a tax levied against an industry that extracts a resource from the ground). Energy producers pay a severance tax in over thirty other states. Not surprisingly, D'Amico said the industry is against paying a severance tax and explained that if he makes a 15 percent profit and has to pay a 5 percent severance tax, then he's only making a 10 percent profit. Making a 10 percent profit is the equivalent of getting back 110 bucks for every 100 bucks spent. That's a good profit, especially if it's multiplied by thousands. My former construction bosses would have loved that kind of profit. D'Amico's answer served purposes other than just flinging around numbers. First, I suspect that the majority of the lessees in the audience assumed that the severance tax would be cutting into landowners' profits as well, which, as I learned later, was not necessarily the case. Second, and more important, D'Amico's response to my question alienated me from many people in the community who had signed leases.[11] He implied that I was willing to take money out of the pockets of people with leases. That makes me a bad guy, one of those "damn tree-huggers."

The local papers showed how the community fractured in late 2008, 2009, and 2010. One person would ask the public to consider the possible risks of environmental degradation that might accompany gas development. Another would respond by dismissing "liberals" who would stop jobs and money from flowing into the area. Granted these were letters to the editor, but they represented much of the conversation about gas. You were either for it or against it. These kinds of simplistic conversations make things easier for the industry, because as long as neighbors aren't talking, the industry can do what it pleases. It can even divide individuals against themselves, as I experienced in a Jekyll/Hyde way, torn between my empathy for people who needed money and my concern about the place where I lived and how I lived there.

Come to find out, D'Amico wasn't being forthright. In the version Pennsylvania governor Ed Rendell proposed (until he took it off the table), the severance tax was basically a 5 percent sales tax at the wellhead, which had been the case in West Virginia since 1987. That means if natural gas sells for $6.40 per thousand cubic feet (Mcf), the state makes $0.32 per Mcf. That's not much, considering that, no matter what precautions it may take, the gas industry will have some negative impact. In addition, the Pennsylvania Budget and Policy Center has stated that wells generally pay for themselves in one or two years, a situation that benefits the gas companies. D'Amico mentioned that the tax would force the gas industry to cut back on employment, language designed to create fear and doubt among local people looking for jobs. What the industry never stated, at least not publicly, is that the gas is not going anywhere, and if they want to drill for it, they have to do it here. Nor does the industry share that much of the Tioga County

Marcellus gas is "sweet gas" or "dry gas," meaning that it comes out of the ground ready to go to market. D'Amico cast me as the bad guy for bringing up a tax that might cut jobs. His response reflected the way the industry crafts its language only to promote the benefits, not to explain the risks.

Even with all the reading I had been doing before the meeting, I found that I did not know enough to challenge the industry's information in any meaningful way. That made me anxious. The academic in me thought the information presented by D'Amico and the others was too favorable to the industry. They raised almost no questions or concerns about gas drilling. I kept thinking, *Wait a friggin' minute! There is no way fracking is as perfect as you make it out to be! That digital video makes fracking look simple, but the places you're drilling are not that neat.*

I found myself wishing for a well-funded group of citizens whose sole purpose was to lobby on behalf of the public health, though I recognized that the public doesn't always have a coherent message it can release through multiple outlets. We needed the kind of access to politicians that many lobbyists have. The industry's example shows that a cohesive message shared through multiple media can be powerfully persuasive, especially when there is not much push-back against it. As one of my friends claimed, "Saying something loudly and boldly over and over makes it true." Many local and state politicians do not want to be questioned about the advantages given to the natural gas industry, because they want the money the gas industry brings in. Around this time, MU's vice president for finance, who had leased his land, told me, "I feel like I've given away my land for $6,700."

The dreamy picture painted by the Wellsboro meeting unsettled me, and my anger about buying in the country intensified.

—◦—

I needed a different perspective and more information, so I looked for meetings in New York. New York was waiting to see what happened in Pennsylvania before unleashing the industry.[12] I found such a meeting in Waverly, New York, held by the Cornell Cooperative Exchange. One balmy July night about two months after the Wellsboro meeting, my buddy Francis, one of the Horses' Asses, and I drove to Waverly. We walked into the elementary school auditorium/gymnasium/cafeteria and noticed right away that, in our early forties, we were two of the youngest people in the crowd. Unlike the soft lights of the Wellsboro auditorium, florescent light bounced off the multipurpose room's cinder-block walls and the chairs' cro-moly tubing and butt-numbing plastic. We listened as academics from Cornell offered a more thorough view of social and environmental concerns based on studies done in Wyoming. One speaker explained to the audience that landowners had considerable power in negotiating their leases, including placing the tax burden on the gas company. I did not hear this information in Wellsboro. Rural sociologist Jeffrey Jacquet stated that residents could expect crime rates to go up as gas development ramped up, an assertion that made the retiree-aged crowd squirm in their seats.

Driving back to Mansfield, Francis and I talked about what we had learned and how it clashed with what we were hearing in our home state. We lamented the lack of consistent information, and I told Francis it made it hard for me to "trust the industry." He agreed. We rode in silence for a few minutes, until our talk turned to beer and bikes.

Later that night I realized the way the audiences responded to the industry revealed insights about the two states. In Wellsboro, the audience was concerned primarily about their leases. In Waverly, the audience was concerned primarily about long-term environmental effects. I cared more about the latter—I wasn't going to buy leased property, and I had read too much Carson and Steingraber to think solely in terms of money. Taken together, the meetings were instructive for the way they gave me a fuller sense of what was happening with the industry and for showing me how public perception and state officials influence the way a place gets used. In Pennsylvania, the message was pro-industry. In New York, the message was "let's see what happens in Pennsylvania." Same shale below, different messages above. If only our words could be as solid as rock. I felt as though we were looking to buy a house on unstable ground.

—○—

As these conflicting messages about the gas industry drilled into my brain, a message of a different sort but no less powerful in its contribution to my unease with buying a house emerged—the university announced that, because of budget shortfalls, it planned to retrench eleven faculty members. "Retrenchment," of course, is bureaucratic-speak for laid off, something a lot of people think can't happen to a tenured professor. It can. The administration saw retrenchment as a way to make up a budget deficit of around $2.7 million. Dated September 14, 2010, the "Mansfield University Plan for Retrenchment" stated that the projected deficit "leaves us at a point where we cannot balance our budget unless we strategically retrench faculty" (Ulrich 2011). Over time the administration realized it could recoup much of the money to cover the shortfall via retirements, fees, and other financial machinations, so it revised the number of retrenchees down to seven. Two of the seven, French professor Monique Oyallon and Spanish professor Fanny Arango-Keeth, were from my department. Close friends from other departments were on the list, including one who had received a grant to test residents' well water for possible contaminants from drilling and to set a baseline for water quality

in the county. My Pabst-drinking and chicken-processing part-
ner, physics professor Mike Chester, appeared on the list. Francis
summed up the situation on one of our rides: "Hell, I'm a tenured,
full professor, and I don't feel safe." As the low man on the totem
pole in my department, neither did I.

The retrenchment plan appeared as we were closing in on a
country house, and the rumors and constantly revised administrative plans making their way around the university stressed me further. The "R" word came up in department meetings, campus-wide
meetings, in the hallways, over beers in the bar, and on bikes out
on the roads. It didn't really matter where faculty were or for what
occasion. Get two or more together and retrenchment was the hot
topic. When Lilace and I argued, I began telling her, "It's stupid to
buy a house when I might lose my job." I worried we were being
irresponsible, and the thought of possibly taking on bigger house
payments and defaulting kept me awake at night. I also thought
about bailing. When a job came open at Western Carolina University, I talked with my chair about applying and asked him for a
letter. He never wrote it though, because I decided, for monetary
and other reasons, to put down roots here.

Most of the words and actions preceding the retrenchment
plan reminded me of what I had read about the industry. The
faculty heard horror stories about what a dire situation our
finances were in, yet we also watched as new positions, like
Assessment Coordinator, were created for people who did not
teach classes and brought in no revenue. According to the
administration, we needed the position to ensure we were reac-
credited, which may have been the case, but it was hard to
believe with all the other uncertainty. Our Division II football program was cut in 2006 because it cost too much, yet we
added a sprint football team in 2008, which I've heard costs
around $400,000 to field, the rough equivalent of four faculty

positions (damned if I can verify that cost). There was talk of private contractors building and staffing new residence halls to attract students, while faculty wondered who would teach them. Such decisions did not soothe the minds of a faculty who were watching their colleagues lose their jobs and being asked to do more and more with less and less.

The irony was not lost on me that the gas industry was spending millions of dollars just off the Mansfield campus while we struggled to keep faculty in the classroom.

—◦—

We kept looking at houses, and I kept thinking buying a house was a bad idea. Part of what fed my anxiety stemmed from an emerging pattern of contradictory metaphors, depending on whether the industry was talking jobs or the environment: the industry as infant and the industry as elder. I didn't see how they could have it both ways. The competing metaphors confused me and made it difficult to understand the impact the industry may have had on buying a home. What to do?

Though I don't recall D'Amico mentioning infants when responding to my question about severance taxes, his answer implies that too much taxation will run the industry off. His statement was a subtle way of saying, "We're a new industry, and we need to make lots of money to stay." The metaphor appeared frequently. The MSC released a statement on its website claiming "Pennsylvania is blessed with rich natural resources, including a potentially large natural gas field in the Marcellus shale. Although the MSC strongly opposes a broad-based severance tax, especially while the development of the Marcellus shale is in its infancy, the industry remains willing to work through the Commonwealth's current financial challenges with the Governor and the legislature" ("Marcellus Shale Committee" 2009).

Stephen Rhoads, president of the Pennsylvania Oil and Gas Association, used the metaphor in a *Harrisburg Patriot-News* editorial titled "Marcellus Shale Tax Won't Solve Budget Woes" (2009): "Pennsylvania's Marcellus Shale industry is still in its infancy. We seem to have the advantage in the current market for investment in shale gas development, and we think it makes good policy sense to keep the balance tipped in our favor. If the proposed severance tax won't make a meaningful contribution to erasing the state's budget deficit, and the lack of such a tax enhances Pennsylvania's competitive position for the capital investment needed to grow new jobs and businesses, will it serve any purpose?"

Pennsylvania politicians relied on the infancy metaphor, a metaphor suggesting a severance tax would crush a growing industry, costing Pennsylvanians jobs and a much-needed economic boost. The metaphor suggested that the public and politicians should take an indulgent stance toward an industry that had not yet learned to walk. We should support innocent growth and development, though the industry played down the need for watching infants closely as they developed, as suggested by D'Amico at the Wellsboro meeting. He said, "The current regulatory climate can be challenging."

When the industry shifted focus from economic to environmental impacts, however, it shifted to the metaphor of the experienced elder. In a July 10, 2009, press release from the MSC website on the proposed Fracturing Responsibility and Awareness of Chemicals Act (FRAC Act),[13] Rhoads claimed that "Hydraulic fracture stimulation has been used in Pennsylvania since 1949. . . . Unnecessary regulation of this practice would hurt our nation's energy security and threaten our economy, and it would destroy Pennsylvania's shallow gas industry" ("PA's Oil, Gas Industry" 2009). Rhoads suggested that natural gas development has a long history in Pennsylvania, which is true, but not natural gas extraction in the form of slickwater hydraulic fracturing practiced now. The industry rarely makes that clear, and the metaphor taps into other concerns by linking regulation with pain/suffering and playing on fear.

Using a similar strategy, Penn State University professor of petroleum and natural-gas engineering Robert W. Watson (2009) claimed in the *Pittsburgh Post-Gazette* that "one thing to keep in mind is that oil and natural-gas development is nothing new to the commonwealth." Watson's editorial discussed the history of hydraulic fracturing, stating that it had its roots in "Pithole City, Pa., circa 1865, and Gulf Oil Co.'s laboratory research of the 1950s." Watson concluded: "But such development is not new. It is not unproven. It is not unsafe." Watson's language echoed Rhoads's and demonstrated how the gas industry, in certain contexts, wanted to alleviate public concerns by arguing that the technology has been used in Pennsylvania for years. *Since 1865! The Civil War was ending, for crying out loud. This stuff is safe.* As I encountered these metaphors, I wondered how the industry could have it both ways. It wanted to be left alone financially because it was a young industry muddling through infancy, struggling to stand, yet when it came to regulation, it wanted to be left alone because it was experienced, the Wise-One-Who-Has-Seen-Everything. Google searches at the time revealed a different story. In places like Wyoming, Colorado, and Texas, environmental mishaps occurred regularly, adding fuel to the flames of my doubts about buying a house. I'm skeptical of history written by interested parties, and the industry appeared to accept its history when it helped and denied it when it didn't. It sounded to me more like a teenager who has learned how to negotiate but lacks impulse control.

Perhaps the most striking feature of Watson's editorial was its insistence on how "important environmental, economic and land-use issues . . . should be robustly debated." I read this and wondered where the hell this debate was taking place. Because the framing of the arguments had been laid out by industry and politicians, I didn't see much in the way of robust debate. Instead, I saw a lot of cheerleading for the industry and random pockets of dissenting voices. I read blogs, articles, and letters in various newspapers, heard speeches of politicians, attended public meetings, and listened to anyone who would talk to me about the industry. In Tioga County, the natural gas industry controlled the agenda and framed the debate.

In 2009 I became a Pine Creek Waterdog, a citizen trained to be part of a watchdog group so I could learn what a gas operation following regulations looked like. The training was designed by land-use planners, watershed management experts, and others for the purpose of offering the financially strapped Department of Environmental Protection (DEP) more eyes on the ground and to prevent the public from clogging DEP phone lines with unnecessary complaints. Our group consisted of teachers, small-business owners, members of Trout Unlimited, college students, and retired college professors. That didn't stop the Pennsylvania Oil and Gas Association (now Pennsylvania Independent Oil and Gas) from labeling us "vigilantes" in a press release, even though it later apologized and removed the post. That's hardly an environment conducive to "robust debate." Yet Watson's choice to portray the debate as "long" and "thorough" contributed to my unease with what I was learning about the industry. Perhaps in Watson's mind the debate was robust, but the gas industry set the terms with its blitzkrieg of trucks and drill rigs. Looking closely at the rhetoric of the gas industry, especially in Tioga County, suggested that there were costs associated with the lack of public debate, though we didn't know what those costs would look like. Too many issues were left unquestioned and uninvestigated. That made investing in property out of town a sketchy proposition for me.

Yet I didn't want to be trapped in town by the industry, and I did want a happy wife. I opened another beer and gritted my teeth. . . .

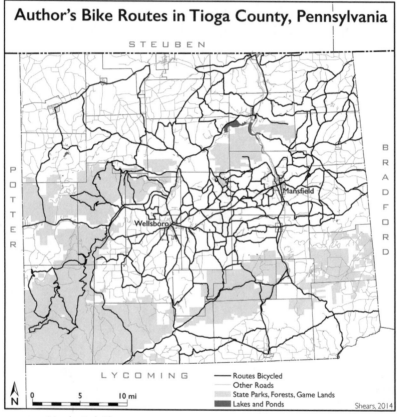

Author's Bike Routes in Tioga County, Pennsylvania

STEUBEN

POTTER

BRADFORD

Mansfield

Wellsboro

LYCOMING

—— Routes Bicycled
—— Other Roads
State Parks, Forests, Game Lands
Lakes and Ponds

0   5   10 mi

N

Shears, 2014

Map by Andy Shears

2   More Than a Blank Space on a Map

✳   I walked out the back door of our house in Mansfield, through the wooden gate, and to the old carriage house that held my bicycles. Since I was heading out on dirt roads, I chose my cyclocross bike, a green and black Jamis that looks like a road bike with knobby tires. I checked the tire pressure, snapped on my helmet, and rode the shared driveway between our house and the frat house next door into the sunshine. Left at the end of the driveway onto Sherwood Street. Pedaled two hundred yards between the Victorian houses that crowd the road to the stop sign. Right onto North Main Street. Hugging the right side of the road, I pedaled past a few houses, the Presbyterian church, the public library, Case's Garage, the Penny Saver office, and the beer distributor. At McDonald's, I looked back for cars. Seeing none, I glided left and took the lane while signaling a left turn into Mansfield's tiny strip mall. At the south end of the mall, Greco's Grocery Store stood dark, out of business. Cars clustered in front of the liquor store, Mr. Stirfry's, the Dollar Store, and CVS. Riding past the Greco's end of the building, I weaved right, then left, then right through the borough shop parking lot and turned right onto the Hike and Bike Trail (HBT), which carried me into the Lambs Creek Recreational Area. The sewage treatment plant ground Mansfield's poop on the left, the levee behind the plant channeling the Tioga River north toward the Tioga Reservoir. The smell of mulch and sewage mingled in the air. The roar of what I guessed were aerators chased me as I pedaled the narrow paved trail past the aluminum-sided buildings toward the boat ramp four miles away. A cemetery and a few houses on the hill scrolled by on my right. A couple hundred yards later, the levee turned east and bisected the HBT at the levee's eastern-most end. I stood and cranked over the small, steep bump, coasted down the backside, and followed the asphalt into the woods.

For me, the HBT serves as an artery to the dirt roads northwest of Mansfield. For others, it's a place to jog, hunt, walk the dogs, or push babies in strollers. I ride it several times a week, though, unlike most of the people who frequent it, I use it as a way to get out of town. It's flat and short, two characteristics that don't satisfy my cycling sensibilities. A path constructed primarily of old road beds (Lambs Creek used to be a village), the HBT stretches through forest and corn fields, the latter leased to farmers by the Army Corps of Engineers. During heavy floods, the fields act as overflow protection. The Tioga River flows north on the west side of the path until it dumps into Tioga Reservoir. On the east side, Highway 15 carries traffic north and south. It's not a big area, hemmed in by river, roads, and residences. One and a half miles past where I crossed the levee, hikers and cyclists can cross the Tioga River via a closed bridge—"What used to be the old road into Mansfield," according to one local—and ride up into the Lambs Creek watershed, the water source for the town. The HBT is not a challenging place to ride a bike—think kids on training wheels and oldsters on comfort bikes. But the HBT makes up for the lack of physical challenge with an abundance of wildness.

On this Friday, I pedaled along late morning, planning to get in a couple of hours of riding before Lilace and the kids got home. It had been a long week teaching, and I needed to sweat and look at some trees. After I crossed the levee, I pedaled past the brackish pond, looking for the great blue heron that hangs out there. No sign. I looked into the American sycamore hanging over the pond, where I once saw a bald eagle sitting on a branch, stoically tolerating an ear-beating from a crow. Today, nothing. I pedaled into a section where the maples, hickories, oaks, and other hardwoods overhung the path, careful to dodge the bone-jarring pothole on the left. On the right side of the path, the ground dipped through a ditch and sloped up toward North Main Street while, on the left, the ground dropped into a mucky bottom filled with saplings, rotting logs, and cattails. The trail stays moist and dark enough here to grow moss on the asphalt.

A couple of minutes later I approached the Highway 15 overpass. Cars clacking on the expansion joints overhead competed with the roar of rapids below the bridge as the path edged toward it. Looking into the distance, I noticed under the overpass two brown shapes trotting away from me. The smaller one trotted behind and to the right of the larger one as they followed the chain-link fence that kept walkers and cyclists out of the river. I stopped pedaling and coasted toward the pair, flipping through my skimpy mental nature guide, trying to figure out what I was seeing when the larger animal paused, whipped its head around, and saw me. Tufted ears came into focus, and I exclaimed, "Holy shit, bobcats!" The bobcat lingered a moment then bolted for a break in the fence.

The adult disappeared under the fence. The cub, lacking the adult's knowledge of its surroundings, did not. It ran a few yards down the fence line, stopped and scrabbled at the chain links with its front paws like it was trying to climb it, saw me getting closer, and dashed further along. The bobcat scrabbled against the fence two more times before it passed the end and disappeared into the honeysuckle and rocks below. Though I felt bad scaring the cub, I exulted at seeing the bobcats. "Damn!" I said. "That was cool! Gotta remember to tell Lilace and the boys at the shop." I replayed the encounter in my head for another one and a half miles, until I crossed the old bridge and started climbing Lambs Creek Road. Then my focus on physical effort—deeper breathing, legs straining to keep a high pedaling cadence—crowded out the image of the cub scratching against the fence.

Though it's bounded by highway, river, and residences, the Lambs Creek Recreation Area has come to represent for me the whole of Tioga County. I've seen deer, snakes, eagles (bald and golden), ospreys, red-tailed hawks, red-winged blackbirds, turkeys, flickers, goldfinches, box turtles, snapping turtles, black bears, and more bobcats, all intermingling in a place used regularly by cyclists, walkers, runners, hunters, students, roller-bladers, and fisherpersons. I've heard gazillions of peepers there. I've ridden the bike path in all four seasons, in 90 degree temps and on subzero days, in sun and rain and snow and wind, morning, afternoon, evening, and night. I've skied it at night in winter, towed my kids on it in a bike trailer in summer. Once my kids and I helped a snapping turtle off the path and into the weeds. Another time, my cycling buddy Tom and I pedaled across the old bridge for points west and spooked a black bear about 30 feet up in a tree. It crashed down the tree like a fireman sliding out of control and smashed off into the underbrush. One spring, after torrential rains, I took the kids around to the Lambs Creek Road side of the HBT so we could walk down to the closed bridge and see how far the Tioga River had risen from its normal level 10 feet below the bottom of the bridge. Mounted on the I-beams crossing the old roadway, the old bridge's signs announced 13'3" of clearance for trucks, and, on this saturated day, the water missed touching the bottom of the sign by inches. When I rode down to the boat ramp a few days later, the water had receded and left enormous blocks of winter ice ten to twelve inches thick and several feet across scattered on the bike path near the Lambs Creek boat ramp.

Over the first three or four years I lived in Mansfield, I began to see the HBT as a barometer for what was happening across the county, and it came to represent for me the way wildness intermingles with civilization here. You can't ignore wildness in Tioga County, which brought to my mind Thoreau's ability to see the wild in the civilized landscape around Walden. Tioga County is a civilized landscape too, but the landscape of farms and industry mingle with state game lands and state forests as wild as any place I've been. Not remote, necessarily, but wild. Though I find other places in Tioga County more beautiful, challenging, and remote for riding than the Lambs Creek Recreation Area, this small patch of wildness fits well into the story I tell myself about the joys of raising a family in a rural area, a place where the land and its wild inhabitants demand attention.

—○—

One reason I see Tioga County as a gift of wildness is because of the attitudes I bring to the place, attitudes shaped in part by my upbringing, my personal history, and what I've learned from books, movies, newspapers, TV shows, and the like. Attitudes can be shaped in two ways: through physical experiences and through the words and images we hear and read. When we contemplate attitudes, we are contemplating an important dimension of the practice of rhetoric, because attitudes are embedded within the words and images we encounter. Any time we encounter words and images, we need to think about them in terms of rhetoric. Kenneth Burke defines rhetoric as "the use of language as a symbolic means of inducing cooperation in beings that by nature respond to symbols" (1950, 43). Rhetoric carries a persuasive function and attempts to achieve its ends through the use of words or images (or both), what Burke calls "symbols." For Burke, one of the key ways rhetoric works is through the crafting of symbolic statements—ads, books, newspaper articles, blogs, policy, films, protests, the Constitution, and so on—that try to accomplish some desired end or persuade people to adopt a certain attitude.

For Burke, any time we communicate via symbols we are experiencing rhetoric. We can't avoid it, in the same way we can't avoid breathing. This doesn't mean that all rhetorical acts are equally true or weighty but that we are dealing with a state of affairs that calls on us to question how the symbols we encounter are being used. Rhetoric functions through the crafting of symbolic statements that tap into attitudes the audience already holds.

Rhetoric tries to tap into attitudes, Burke tells us, because attitudes are "incipient acts" (1945, 235–47). By that, he means that our attitude about something predisposes us to act in certain ways or to desire certain things. Lilace's and my attitudes about moving to the country are useful here. Generally, we shared the same attitude about extractive industries: we distrusted them. Where we differed was our approach toward dealing with the problem. I thought we were safer in town, because I figured that the last thing the industry wanted was headlines blaring "Giant Gas Company Poisons Town's Water." Lilace thought we'd be able to monitor our water more carefully out of town, because we weren't relying on others to do it for us. Same attitude, same distrust, different perspective on how to handle the risk. It gets more complicated. We each saw our house in town in a different way. I didn't spend much time there and I slept through the drunk students, so I saw it as a refuge. Lilace spent a lot of time there, and she began to see it as a prison. It didn't help that college boys lived around us, loud parties occurred frequently, and we had a super-social daughter. Both of us were concerned about the same things, yet our arguments about whether to buy a house depended on how we saw our daily lives in the house.

We can choose not to act, of course, but often we act in accordance with our attitudes. In fact, Burke would go so far as to argue that attitudes are symbolic actions; that is, attitudes can be seen as representing a physical act because they contain the impulse that drives a physical act. Attitudes predict what we are most likely to do and how we are most likely to talk about something. I'd rather ride my bike than go hunting, but I'm willing to kill chickens to avoid buying meat in Styrofoam trays. Though simplistic, these examples are instructive for the way they show how attitudes can motivate us to act. This is not to say we always do what our attitudes suggest we might want to. I have a bad attitude about meetings, and I often don't want to go to them, but I go anyway. My responsibilities compel me to. Given the freedom to choose, however, I am more likely to act in ways that align with my attitudes, what some might call "pursuing my bliss"—hence my wife's and my excitement at moving to rural Pennsylvania in the first place. Lilace and I saw the school and the place as containing possibilities that aligned with attitudes about nature and wildness we already held.

Attitudes are involved any time humans, acting individually or collectively as an industry, political party, or other aligned group, attempt to create something. So we have to ask ourselves: What is the effect of holding attitudes? What happens when attitudes conflict? The convergence of disparate attitudes is a feature of rhetoric that complicates things, because attitudes stem from different motivations and desires. For instance, I tend to idealize nature and want to preserve it, so I tell stories about seeing bobcats, because the stories contain attitudes that I hold dear and, I hope, persuade others to think like me or, at least, consider my ideas. If we think of the gas industry as a "person," something not so hard these days, given Supreme Court ruling in *Citizens United*,[1] we can see that the industry holds certain attitudes as well. Whereas I would want to preserve the HBT as a bobcat habitat, the natural gas industry might see it as a place where natural gas should be extracted.[2] The idea of a bobcat habitat doesn't enter its equation as strongly, if at all. The industry prioritizes action that focuses on jobs or supplying America with gas while making a profit. Because that's the case, the attitudes that motivate gas industry participants often clash with mine.

To make things even more complicated, rhetoric works in such a way that it tries to tap into the attitudes we already hold, either to change them or to maintain them, depending on the motivations of the speaker or writer. In our case, Lilace and I wanted to live in a rural area because we value nature and wildness. It fits with our belief that Wordsworth had it right when he complained, "The world is too much with us." The gas industry is a part of that world.

—○—

Lilace and I sold our house in Reno and moved to Mansfield in 2005 because I was offered a job as an assistant professor of English and Director of Composition at Mansfield University (MU). I chose the job for the usual reasons: paycheck with benefits, closer to family, and, well, I needed to work. Some of our reasons for moving to Mansfield, like being closer to family or getting a paycheck, had little to do with the physical place itself being desirable. All jobs would have fulfilled at least one of those requirements. But we desired to live in a rural place, a desire that grew out of the way we valued interacting with nature and wildness. We shared an impulse to live a twenty-first century pastoral idyll.

MU understood the pull of the pastoral. The job ad described the university as "located within Tioga County, home to five state and federal parks, seven lakes, and the 50-mile long gorge of the Pennsylvania Grand Canyon. The university is an hour south of the Finger Lakes wine region of upstate New York." The ad echoed passages from books like *A Sand County Almanac*, though maybe not as gracefully, and tapped into our experiences of other places we'd lived and stories we'd been reading and telling ourselves about where we wanted to settle. Unlike many academics, our desire to live in a small town close to farms and forests outweighed our desire for access to museums and musicals. Because of our desire, one of my dissertation committee members called us "weird" for preferring the nature of the farm and the woods to the urban culture of the mind and books (we see the rural as culture too). We wanted to live in a place where we could buy our food locally and have a garden. We believed we needed to lead quiet lives close to the land, as close as academics with few such skills can anyway, and we hoped that connecting with farms and farmers would educate us in another rich culture. We wanted a place we could connect to through our brains and our stomachs.

Since Tioga County sits at the northern end of the Appalachian mountain range, the oldest mountain range in the United States, I felt another connection that grew from my time in the Appalachians of North Carolina. I liked knowing that the mountains I eat from and teach, pedal, and write in extended 600 miles south to a place I've spent much of my forty-seven years. I was born in North Carolina, and much of my family still lives in the western part of the state. As kids, my brother and I used to summer with our grandparents in Banner Elk, extended visits that meant climbing the mountains and wading the creeks with our cousins. As an undergrad at Appalachian State and later a resident of Beech Mountain, I spent hundreds of days in the southern Appalachians hiking, paddling, cycling, rock climbing, and sitting on rock outcroppings drinking beer or tequila. Those behaviors continue in the northern Appalachians, a long-range connection I find comforting.

—◦—

Like many people, my love for the outdoors grew early. I joined the Boy Scouts as a Cub Scout and stayed in until I was eighteen, becoming an Eagle Scout along the way. As a teen, I camped out several times a year with my scout troop, experiences that lent themselves to my desire to learn to rock climb as an undergraduate at Appalachian State University. After college, I backpacked, raced my mountain bike, climbed more rocks, and surfed. When I met Lilace, she was making choices that kept her outside as well, via backpacking, kayaking, and teaching English and environmental studies at the Outdoor Academy of the Southern Appalachians. I can be perfectly content sitting with a book for an entire day, a prerequisite for an English prof, but I get twitchy if I don't get outside on a regular basis and work over my body. I need the trees, the animals, and the movement through a landscape that snaps me out of my academic preoccupations and reminds me there is more to this world than words.

My sense of the world was shaped in part by my truck-driving father. My grandfather and his brothers owned a trucking company. I began taking trips on eighteen-wheelers when I was five years old. For my first truck trip, family friend Mike Greene took me from Charlotte to Raleigh, North Carolina. I told my mom when I got home, "I'm a real truck driver. I peed on a tire." I took trips with Daddy from age five until after I graduated college. I enjoyed moving through the landscape in a truck, seeing Pittsburgh's steel mills or a nuclear sub leaving the Chesapeake Bay. I enjoyed sleeping in the truck, the roar of the diesel lulling me for ten hours at a stretch. Around nineteen, I realized that I was getting the gift of uninterrupted time with Daddy. I quit sleeping so much, deciding that if he was awake, I was awake. That meant some long hours—on one trip, we drove to Northville, Michigan (basically, west Detroit), then to Louisville, Kentucky, then to Peoria, Illinois, where we picked up a load of "slinkys"—big coils of steel used for manufacturing concrete reinforcing wire—then to Memphis, Tennessee, and home to Charlotte, North Carolina. We were gone over four days, and I think we slept about five hours a day, though we got one good night's sleep in a hotel. We filled the time talking about school, girls, family, sports, and shitty drivers. Sometimes we'd just ride, looking at the world unfurl past the window of the Freightliner. That I now love moving through landscapes on a bicycle makes sense.

No matter where we were or what we were doing, however, if Daddy saw a red-tailed hawk, he pointed it out. Always. We might be in the midst of talking about how that idiot in the Mazda should have his license revoked or how Junior Hicks burned to death in a truck crash after dodging a car or whether Darrell Waltrip was a better NASCAR driver than Buddy Baker or the time my brother left his favorite hat in a terminal in St. Louis. In the midst of the story, Daddy's hand would shoot out: "Look at that hawk." The hawk may be 75 yards off the side of the interstate, barely discernible among the branches, but there it was. We may see five in an hour, perched on tree branches and telephone poles or surfing air currents. He pointed out every hawk we passed, as well as peregrines, ospreys, the occasional bald eagle, and other raptors. I always looked.

Over time I came to understand "Look at that hawk" as a lesson in seeing. Look outside the lines, Daddy seemed to be saying. Get outside the boundaries of what's human. There's a lot to see out there, and it's damn amazing. Rhetoric works in a similar way. It asks us to think about the boundaries of words and images. Words and images can keep our attention inside the lines of our thinking, or they can help us look outside those lines.

—◦—

I carried Daddy's lesson of looking outside the lines with me when I started working construction for a general contractor, Omni Southeast, Inc., after I graduated from App State. A glorified gofer at first, I worked my way into superintending jobs, mostly for grading contracts. I traveled a lot and learned new things, namely that my main job involved dealing with people and cleaning up messes. One of my biggest attitude adjustments from this period came in the cab of an International TD-15 bulldozer. In that dozer, I finally understood the seductive power of power.

One of our jobs involved raising a dam outside of York, South Carolina. Omni hired Eggers Construction from Banner Elk, North Carolina, to do the grading. One day I drove from my company's Charlotte office about forty minutes south to the job site to check on the work. When I arrived, I pulled up beside Eddie Eggers, the sub's boss, as he looked at blueprints. Eddie had known Daddy for years, and Eddie and I had become drinking buddies. I rolled down my window. "What's going on?"

Eddie looked at me. "You ever run a dozer?"

"No."

"Well, it ain't hard. I'll show you." Turns out Eddie was short an operator, and he needed someone to clear trees in the borrow area, the place where they "borrowed" dirt to raise the dam. We walked over to the International TD-15, where he then gave me instructions on how to raise and lower the blade, go forward and backward (you let off a pedal to accelerate a dozer), left and right, and sent me across the dam to push down trees. I clattered across, worried that I was going to steer the dozer into the water or roll it down the downstream side of the dam. A TD-15 is a big dozer with a blade about three feet high and eight feet wide.

Once I clack-clack-clacked across the dam, I turned toward the trees, most of which were between 40 and 80 feet tall. Over the next two hours, I pushed down and cleared away twenty or so trees, cutting the roots on one side with the corner of the blade, backing down between trees in order to push them out toward the newly cleared area (to avoid creating a tangle of downed trees), driving straight up onto the tree as far as I could (dared!) until the tree leaned precipitously; then I backed off, lowered the blade, and drove forward, catching the root ball with the blade and popping the tree out of the ground. Trees that had been growing for thirty, forty, fifty years—bam!—felled in minutes. I found that I relished the work, the roar of the diesel (much louder than Daddy's truck), the clatter of the tracks, the idea of controlling something much more powerful than me.

Although I've always preferred bicycles to diesels, the lesson I learned that day sank deep into my psyche. Big machines make humans feel powerful, and they give us power all out of proportion to what we are physically capable of. The dozer made me feel powerful in a world bigger than me, something I'd never understood so clearly before. Daddy understood it perfectly. He told me once, only half in jest, "Hell, in my twenties, I would have driven a truck for free." He felt that power in his bones. While I enjoyed my day on the dozer, my experience of that power clashed with my desire to leave nature untouched. I felt as though I'd accomplished something big—I pushed down trees!—yet the experience pushed my attitude further in the direction of preserving it. Big machines make it too easy not to.

Coupled with my experience on the dozer, Daddy's lesson in seeing outside the lines rattled through my head when I went back to college for a second bachelor's degree and graduate school. Through a series of fortunate events, I began to read nature writing and study environmental rhetoric. I sensed that, by making ourselves more powerful than we really are, humans hold attitudes that may doom us. The study of nature writing and rhetoric meshed with attitudes about nature I already held and helped me see further outside Daddy's lines. I began to think more deeply about my relationship to nature, what I valued, and how I might preserve both. One important aspect of that preservation, I was to learn, involved language.

—◦—

While earning a master's degree in English at Western Carolina University (WCU) from 1997 to 1999, the genre of nature writing brought much of my scattered thinking together while pushing me to see outside the lines. Daddy's lesson made more sense, my dismay at the destruction wrought by construction gained a frame, and my desire to be outdoors took on a fuller history and meaning. Though the texts I encountered are too numerous to recount, they reinforced and reshaped my attitudes toward the natural world and my relationship with it by simultaneously reinforcing and challenging what I thought.

Two books I encountered that stand out were Gary Snyder's (1990) *The Practice of the Wild* and Richard Nelson's (1995) *The Island Within*. In Snyder's book, I encountered such phrases as "The word *wild* is like a grey fox trotting off through the forest, ducking behind bushes, going in and out of sight" (9). I wasn't sure what Snyder meant by this topic sentence that led into an extended etymology and definition of "wild," but I was drawn to the physicality and immediacy of the image. The phrase reminded me of moments I had experienced, like seeing a red-tail dive, and helped me attach meaning to them beyond "Holy shit!" I embraced his statement, "Our bodies are wild" (16) and tried to explain it to my students as that moment when you're walking through town on a crystal-clear day and for whatever reason— love, the smell of honeysuckle and cut grass, the sight of a red- tailed hawk—joy bursts through your suddenly quivering, buoyant body, causing you to almost skip. Bouncing on my toes, I'd ask a class full of blank faces: "Don't you feel that sometimes?"

Snyder influenced the way I thought about home too. He writes: "Our place is part of what we are" (1990, 27). I carried this line with me as I thought back over extended visits to my grandparents' home in the North Carolina mountains. I saw the rocks I climbed as doing more than simply providing me with a cool way to spend my day. They were shaping me, the tiny finger-holds forcing the muscles in my forearms to grow. The idea that place literally shaped me gobsmacked me and pushed me further outside the lines of what I ordinarily thought.

Now my attitudes while at WCU seem overly romanticized (though it was a pretty romantic time given that Lilace and I were falling in love). Because I was into nature, the books I read reinforced my attitudes and helped me to explain them to myself. Snyder's *The Practice of the Wild* pushed me further down a path I was already walking. To put it in Burke's terms, Snyder persuaded me to act more forcefully on attitudes I already held. My attitudes influenced the way I read literature at WCU too and resulted in a thesis claiming that, in Tennyson's *Idylls of the King*, Arthur's court disintegrated because Arthur's conception of purity did not account for "the fact that humans are an intrinsic part of the dynamic system of nature"[3]—in other words, *wild. The Practice of the Wild* made me see wildness everywhere.

Snyder's ideas about wildness helped me understand certain attitudes I held, validated them, and placed them in a larger context. Richard Nelson's *The Island Within* did the same, while pushing me to question some of my attitudes about humans interacting with nature and leading me to adopt different ones. Sometimes Nelson echoed Snyder: "There is nothing in me that is not of earth, no split instant of separateness, no particle that disunites me from the surroundings. I am no less than the earth itself. The rivers run through my veins, the winds blow in and out with my breath, the soil makes my flesh, the sun's heat smolders inside me. A fouled molecule that runs through the earth runs through me. Where the earth is cleansed and nourished, its purity infuses me. The life of the earth is my own. My eyes are the earth gazing at itself" (1995, 249). Like Snyder, Nelson tries to get the reader to see how humans are not separate from nature but an intrinsic part of it—how places are a part of who we are. It's a powerful notion, one that speaks of connectedness and drives questions I ask often in class, like "Are we nature?"

But Nelson's ideas challenged my attitudes in ways that Snyder's did not. My biggest attitude adjustment stemmed from Nelson's ideas about hunting and eating, based on what he learned during his anthropological study of Koyukon people in Alaska. His research challenged attitudes he held about hunting and challenged mine, which were, basically: don't hunt. I preferred my wild animals alive. Not that I had any experience with hunting. My family did not hunt. We fished occasionally, and we were willing to eat wild game, but none of us spent time sighting in a scope for deer season. I formed my attitudes about hunting based on a few articles I read in the *Outdoor Life* magazines my grandfather used to get (I never knew why—he didn't hunt) and what I saw in the news or out in the woods on hikes and bike rides. Over time, I adopted an attitude about hunting that was based on the barest minimum of knowledge. I quoted Edward Abbey as a defense: "I'm a humanist; I'd rather kill a *man* than a snake" (1968/1990, 17).

As I read *The Island Within*, my attitude toward hunting changed considerably. Nelson's story revolves around what he learned about Koyukon culture. Since the Koyukon live in Alaska, they rely on hunting for much of their food. *The Island Within* explores Nelson's grappling with the natives' ideas toward nature and animals, especially in terms of hunting, and how he tries to incorporate their beliefs into his own life in Alaska. His studies led him to see animals offering themselves as gifts to a hunter who is in harmony with the world. The record of his struggle between the pull of native culture and Western culture challenged me to rethink my assumption that hunting must be bad because it destroyed the very thing—nature—that Daddy and Snyder taught me to appreciate.

Nelson tries his best to fit the idea of a successful hunt into the framework the Koyukon taught him—the deer gives itself as a gift, an act that must be treated respectfully. At one point, breaking from a close description of a doe he sees during a hunt, Nelson leaves the reader in suspense, recalling something a Koyukon elder told him: "Grandpa William often spoke of a rightness in this: the meeting of hunter and prey foreordained, a willful exchange of life, a manifestation of willful power, in a watchful world where little happens purely by chance. Looking at the deer, I can sense again the wisdom of his oft-repeated phrase: 'Every animal knows way more than you do'" (1995, 26). Such statements conflicted with the view of hunting I held, which was basically that hunters took what they wanted with no sense of reciprocity or exchange: a guy with a gun dropping a beautiful animal, sometimes just to hang on the wall. The notion of bagged game as a gift? That idea opened all kinds of questions about issues like acknowledging where our food comes from and recognizing that humans and animals share this world in ways I hadn't considered, a point driven home when Nelson writes, "I am the deer and the deer is me" (249). Though I still had no desire to run out and buy a .30–06, I began to see in a limited way that there could be more to hunting than simply killing something beautiful.

Not long after I read *The Island Within*, I read Nelson's (1997) *Heart and Blood: Living with Deer in America*. *Heart and Blood* covers the gamut of human/deer interactions in the United States, ranging from hunting season (hunting from stands and drives) to overpopulation of deer in urban areas to ranches dedicated to trophy hunting to shooting deer to protect crops. I read sentences like "Whenever any of us sit down for breakfast, lunch, dinner, or a snack, it's likely that deer were killed to protect some of the food we eat and the beverages we drink. This is true for everyone: city dwellers and suburbanites; men, women, and children; omnivores and vegetarians; hunters, non-hunters, and anti-hunters" (310). The chapter titled "Opening Weekend" made me think more carefully about the social and cultural value of deer hunting. The image of yahoos with guns I carried in my head morphed into a different image of hunting. Perhaps more important, my attitude about eating changed as well, and I realized my tendency to idealize nature had to account for the fact that animals (and plants) died so that I could live. I had gone from holding attitudes about nature that were primarily aesthetic to understanding that I was as much a part of natural processes as the hawks and deer. I now peered way outside my lines.

I read Snyder and Nelson while attending graduate school at WCU. During my master's studies and later at the doctoral program in English at the University of Nevada, Reno, I read more texts like Snyder's and Nelson's, books that tapped into attitudes I was predisposed toward while growing my understanding of why my attitudes were relevant, even necessary, during the environmental crises of the twentieth and early twenty-first centuries. You could say that my world got a lot bigger (which is exactly what grad school is supposed to do). Some of the books were popular, like Barry Lopez's *Arctic Dreams* (1986), Abbey's *Desert Solitaire* (1968), and Sandra Steingraber's *Living Downstream* (1997).[4] Some of the books were classics, like Henry David Thoreau's *Walden* (1854) and Rachel Carson's *Silent Spring* (1962). Some were academic: Cheryl Glotfelty and Harold Fromm's *The Ecocriticism Reader: Landmarks in Literary Ecology* (1996), Paul Shepard's *Man in the Landscape* (1967), and Joseph Meeker's *The Comedy of Survival* (1972). I read Darwin's *Voyage of the Beagle* (1839) and *Origin of Species* (1859) and David Ehrenfeld's *The Arrogance of Humanism* (1978). Some defied categories, like John Elder's *Read-*

ing the Mountains of Home (1998). I was introduced to environmental rhetoric through M. Jimmie Killingsworth's and Jacqueline Palmer's *Ecospeak: Rhetoric and Environmental Politics in America* (1992), Carl Herndl's *Green Culture* (1996), and too many academic articles to count. I met various writers and academics like Snyder, Lopez, John Elder, Wendell Berry, Terry Tempest Williams, Bill McKibben, Michael Cohen, and environmental historian Richard White. I learned about the environmental issues facing the world, like climate change (then known as global warming), deforestation, mountaintop-removal coal mining, and the problems accompanying the disposal of nuclear waste. Although I spent a lot of time outside rock climbing and riding my bike, I realize now that most of what I learned about nature and environmental issues came from drilling into the issues via words. I found myself agreeing with some ideas, disagreeing with others, rejecting this, adopting that, and I recognized that all these texts resonated with attitudes about nature I learned from my earlier days looking at red-tail hawks from the window of a Freightliner and climbing rocks.

—◦—

I carry the attitudes shaped by all I've read and heard about nature with me every time I pedal a bike in Tioga County. My attitudes are a permanent part of my equipment, like my helmet, water bottle, and flat-repair kit. My encounters with language concerning nature serve as a means of focusing my attention and influencing my reactions to what I see. I see a bobcat, and I value it for its wildness. I want to preserve it instead of hang the skin on the wall, something many people around here would like to do. I learn more about this place pedaling through it at speeds controlled by geography and physical effort instead of an accelerator. Traveling at 70 mph on the truck with Daddy gave me a chance to see a lot, but I didn't *feel* what I saw in the same way I do when climbing a hill at 8 mph, which tells me the hill inclines at a 6 to 8 percent gradient, or pedaling through rain in mid-thirties temps, which tells me I'm damn cold. You can't learn from the seat of a car or truck that mid-twenties temps and snow can be warmer than mid-thirties and rain. In a car or a truck, we can forget we are animals.

Over time I've begun to think of bike riding as a form of reading that shapes my attitudes as much as it shapes my legs. Roads and trails become the equivalent of texts. Short solo rides are like a dip into a magazine, newspaper, or blog. A group ride, like Wednesday's Man Night, is like a short story or essay. A century, cyclist-speak for a 100-mile day, equals a book. On those rare weeks where I crank out between 200 and 400 miles in four or five days, my time in the saddle becomes the equivalent of digging into Eliot's *Middlemarch* or Dickens's *Our Mutual Friend*. Like most reading experiences, my rides serve as an escape and an engagement, a time to think about issues or concerns more deeply or a time to leave them behind like sweat dripping off my elbows and the end of my nose. Because of this, withholding riding from me is like withholding beer or books—I get twitchy, irritable, and uneasy. To keep those feelings at bay, I ride. And I ride to understand the place I live, to make it a part of me.

—◦—

A chilly September rain streaks the windows when I roll out of bed at 5:00 a.m. on Sunday. Mansfield is quiet. I pull on shorts and sweatshirt in the dark, feel my way downstairs to the kitchen, and flip on the light. First order of business: coffee. Pot on, I chug a pint of water and rummage through the cabinet for some Cheerios wannabes called Honey Nut Scooters. I pour a bowl and walk into the dining room to eat. I look out the three big bay windows toward the college student rental house 30 feet away. I won't miss that view if we move out of town. As soon as it's light enough, I'll take my cross bike out for a 50-some-mile ride west to the Tioga State Forest near Asaph. Cereal finished, I walk back into the kitchen, fill a coffee mug, and eat a banana. I think about eating a bagel. My ride will last over four hours, and I will burn a lot of calories. I drink more water and, as all cyclists facing a long ride do, hope to shit soon.

Bathroom affairs in order, I fill water bottles and creep back upstairs to my office to change into my Lycra shorts and jersey. I pull on arm warmers and a vest, grab my spare tube, Clif bars, ID, helmet, and cycling shoes, and tip-toe back downstairs and out into the morning gray at 6:40 a.m. Fortunately, the rain has slowed to a drizzle. I'll get wet, but not soaked, which makes it easier to leave the house. Through the gate, back to the carriage house, I pump up the tires, snap on the helmet, pedal down the driveway, and turn toward the HBT. The streets are quiet, except for the hiss of my tires against the wet pavement. I watch the spray spin up in front of the handlebars and try to avoid puddles. Water beads on my vest. I pass the occasional beer can or Solo cup in the gutter, artifacts from the previous night's college parties. No one stirs. Too early for church. Not even the birds are singing.

Past McDonald's, I turn into the mall parking lot and weave my way to the HBT. Past the sewage treatment plant. Over the levee. Past the heron's pond and the cattails. I cross the closed bridge, turn right on Lambs Creek, and leave the HBT behind. It will be around 11:00 a.m. when I see it again.

I climb Lambs Creek Road's gentle grade toward the Lambs Creek water wells, near the head of Lambs Creek. Where the creek passes under the road, water roars more loudly than usual due to the rain. I have not seen another living soul, unless you believe dairy cows have souls. A couple of minutes later, I bear right on

Shaw Road, passing Firetower Road. Firetower climbs 1,000 feet in two miles, making it one of Tioga County's burliest climbs for cyclists. I've climbed its graveled surface several times, and I remember well its 10 to 12 percent grades at the bottom, the false flat in the middle, and the gradients of over 12 percent coupled with "No Winter Maintenance" road conditions at the top half. I've seen Jack-in-the-pulpits almost two feet tall about a quarter of the way up on the left, where the creek runs beside the road for a few hundred yards. One day driving up for a picnic with the kids, Lilace and I saw a bobcat cross the road in front of us. On one bike ride, I was stopped by a hunter who warned me of a momma bear with two cubs just below the upper section of the road. He said she bared and clacked her teeth at him as a warning to get lost. I rode up anyway that day, though I was a little jumpy. I keep pedaling on Shaw, my bike computer telling me I'm 20 minutes out of Mansfield.

I turn right on Carpenter Road and begin climbing in earnest. The few houses I pass are set back into the woods too far to see. Driveways and mailboxes give them away. Hardwoods hang over the road for the next half mile, until I crest the hill onto a false flat. I pass one of my favorite houses in the county—a modest ranch with a plywood silhouette of a moose standing in the yard and a small garden across the road. The trees recede from the road and frame corn fields on the left and marshland replete with a small pond on the right. I love the perfect hawk habitat southwest of the house, and I often see red-tails sitting on telephone poles or surfing the air currents. The pond hosts red-wing blackbirds every summer. Leaving that terrain behind, I pedal up the two short, steep grades that mark the end of climbing on Carpenter, drop back down past more cornfields, a house and barn, and more marshland until I connect with Park Road, which marks the northern boundary of Hills Creek State Park.

—o—

The next big climb is Reese Hill Road. Like most climbs around here, it's short—less than ten minutes—but steep. The road climbs straight up the side of Reese Hill. Few fields here. Trees hang over the road, except when broken up by the occasional yard or gas pipeline right-of-way. I pedal up at 5 mph. The hill is too steep and I'm too big (195 pounds) to climb it much faster, though I could if I wanted to hurt. Since I am only about an hour into my ride, I ride the hill slower than I normally do, knowing that going hard now will hurt two hours later. My goal is to get to the top without losing control of my breathing. If I can do that, it means I am in shape, which means it's fall, which means I piled on miles all summer, climbing dozens of hills.

As I pedal up, I keep my breathing in control (I'm in shape!), look for deer, and catalog what I know of this hill. At the bottom on the right, just where the hill steepens, wild leeks (in North Carolina we call these ramps) grow in abundance. I've seen deer on the left and right side of the road, once spooking a four-point buck who didn't hear or smell me. Alerted by my tires crunching gravel, he crashed off through the trees quicker than I suspected he could. I stop at the pipeline right-of-way two-thirds of the way up and watch deer feed in the distance near a homemade deer blind. Two studied me a minute, white tails flicking, before returning to their browse. I wondered how long it takes deer to figure out they need to stay away from the blind during deer season.

—o—

Before reaching the top of Reese Hill Road, I turn right on Ikes Road. I climb the short rise past my buddy Eric's property on the left and bomb down the hill past the occasional house and yard carved into the trees. Right onto Catlin Hollow Road. A half mile later, left onto Muck Road. At the Y, I veer right, pass a cemetery, cross the railroad tracks and Highway 287, and pedal straight on Norris Brook Road. After four miles of Norris Brook's 2 to 3 percent grade past houses and camps, I turn left at an old barn onto Spoor Hollow Road, cross Norris Brook, and climb into Tioga State Forest.

Spoor Hollow rises west through hardwoods and evergreens on the northern side of the Tioga State Forest section locals call Asaph. Due to the trees hanging over it, the gravel road is always dark and slightly damp. On this Sunday, it is wet. Rain drips from the trees, and my tires sink into the sticky surface. Moss grows on the rocks balanced beside drainage ditches, and, during summer, red efts wriggle across the road. The road is always quiet, though occasionally I hear the jungle call of a far-off northern flicker or the chitter of concerned chipmunks. Spoor Hollow is not a steady climb but a series of steep steps, each followed by a gentler grade, thus requiring maximum effort followed by what passes for rest. Climbing the road is like reading short, exclamatory sentences interspersed with medium, declarative ones. About halfway up, Stinger Trail intersects Spoor Hollow on the right. Stinger leads straight up the side of the mountain, a washed-out gully of a trail containing loose rocks and roots that climbs past hickories, maples, dogwoods, and other hardwoods. Too steep to ride up (but a feared descent among local mountain bikers), Stinger connects Spoor Hollow to the stunning Plantation Trail, a rolling romp through the woods with just enough rocks, roots, and log crossings to keep things interesting.

I turn onto Stinger, spinning on the wet roots at the bottom and bouncing across more on the short, flat section that leads to the base of the climb proper. I half-heartedly accelerate up the steepening hill, knowing that if I dig too deep into oxygen debt here, the uphill hike-a-bike will hurt that much worse. The slope stops my bike, and I step off. Shouldering my bike, I slog up the hill, looking at the muddy trail for solid footing among the loose rocks, sometimes using roots as steps. Water drips from the trees, and I slip in the mud, weaving back and forth across the trail, pushing off nearby trees. Loose rocks slide under my feet, while my bike frame cuts into my shoulder and knocks my helmet over my eyes. I have slogged up this hill enough to know that slower is faster, and I take smaller steps to lighten the workload on my muscles. Soon, my breathing accelerates, sweat drips off my nose, and my quads burn. There's nothing easy about this climb—there never is—though I tell myself riding Plantation in this misty, cloudy weather will be worth it.

At the top, I drop my bike, the chain rattling against the derailleur, take a swig from my water bottle, and press my helmet against my forehead to force the sweat out of the pads, watching it drip into the mud. After my breathing returns to normal, I throw a leg over the bike and push off, pedaling up the last 100 yards of Stinger to where it intersects Plantation Trail. I hop my bike over small logs extending across the trail—three to be exact—and follow the trail around a slick 90-degree bend onto Plantation Trail proper.

About two miles long, Plantation Trail follows the ridgeline west to the top of Straight Run Road. It's super fun and super beautiful on a bike, or on foot, and though you can't really see into the distance because of the trees, it's on one of the tallest ridges in Tioga State Forest, cresting out at a little over 2,300 feet. On sunny days, there's a sense that you're up there via glimpses of sky and horizon through the trees. Today the sky hangs heavy and close over the trail.

I pedal up an easy grade and across several rock steps. The ground slopes down on my left, up on my right, and reminds me of old forest roads cut into the sides of mountains. Tall, wet grass scrapes my shoes and the occasional sapling scratches my leg. Plantation could follow an old logging road for all I know, a remnant from the logging industry. Given its state forest designation, I thought I would never encounter any sort of extractive industry, though I would learn differently in time.

I follow the winding, rolling, single track across the ridge, bursting through spider webs, past the place where I scared a doe one day, past the bend where I saw a lone Indian pipe, or ghost plant, and over the log crossing that used to intimidate me. Mountain laurel mingle with red and white oaks and beech trees, and in one section of trail near the west end, I pedal into a hemlock stand, tires silent on the damp brown needles. I descend a short, rocky slope, rocks clattering against my rims, tires slipping in the mud, and weave through a section where the understory recedes and large trees dominate. The trail carves through moss and plunges down another short, rocky slope into a rocky, rooty section that ends at the top of Straight Run Road. I look both ways for traffic, even though I know I am unlikely to see any, and pedal across Baldwin Run Road to bomb Straight Run Road's four-mile descent through the forest to the US Geological Survey's National Fishery Research Laboratory in the town of Asaph.

I pedal through the four-way stop that marks the main intersection in Asaph, a collection of houses and the lab, and turn onto the Pine Creek Rail Trail toward home, about 25 miles away. If I'm lucky, I will see a great blue heron wading along Marsh Creek, a swampy area on the south side of the Rail Trail. Or perhaps I will spot another Baltimore oriole, though I doubt it in this weather.

Six miles later, I connect with my earlier route at Muck Road. Tracing my earlier route in reverse, I turn left onto Sherwood Street an hour and thirty minutes later and pedal slowly to the house, thinking about a beer, a shower, and some warm food. I had ridden about 54 miles, and I believed I deserved all three.

—○—

I've taken hundreds of rides similar to this one since I've lived in Tioga County, riding over 8,000 miles the first three years I lived here. Two things jump out at me about these rides. First, I ride past many houses and other signs of human development, but I never focus on them the way I do the animals and the trees. When I find a road or a trail that punches through what scientists call Appalachian Oak Forest or Northern Hardwood Forest, representing the two dominant types of forest in this part of Pennsylvania, I look closely at the trees—oaks, birches, beeches, maples, hemlocks. Well, I look at the blur of them, since I move through the trees too fast to identify them, but I'm left with a sense that there's a lot. It's no accident that timber was, and is, an important industry in Penn's woods. Pedaling past miles and miles of the silvery trunks of oaks, the mottled bark of sycamores, the peeling white of birches, and the rich browns of hemlocks reminds me that there's a life-force here that's bigger than me. Being among the trees mellows me, knocks the edge off whatever work or home stress I carry with me any given day. I expect nature to chill me out, an expectation that stems partly from the attitudes I hold. (I know people who do not find nature relaxing at all.)

I arrived here in part by reading respectful accounts of nature that portray it as a place people go to relax, to regroup, to recreate themselves. In *The Decay of Lying*, Oscar Wilde (1889/1995) declares that artists painting fog is what caused people to see fog. While I'm not sure I buy that completely, Wilde's point that we see or pay attention to what symbols tell us to see fits with the idea that words direct our attention toward certain things and downplay others. Naming works the same way. You can't see something until it's named, so you don't know if you lose it. I have yet to read a book that waxes poetic about the beauties of houses scattered along a back road, so I don't pay much attention to houses. That doesn't mean such a book isn't out there (architectural magazines come to mind). It just means I haven't seen it, nor am I likely to. But I've read millions of words about nature and trees. Those words direct me the way a road or a trail does.

Though much of what I pass on the bike is a blur, a stream of trees from which the occasional leaf or trunk of a red or white oak or hickory pops into focus, I connect physically to the place because I absorb its geography into my body. My pedaling defines the watersheds, roads, creeks, and hills, and I imprint the landscape with images of wildlife or rare plants when and where I encounter them. Tioga County is a civilized landscape, but I don't see as clearly the civilized part of the county when I ride my bike, mostly because I'm not looking for it. Given the presence of the forests and mountains around here, the signs of human civilization can appear tenuous, as exemplified by the old church on Hills Creek Road that's decaying and covered in vines, or the ruins of the lumber town, Landrus, south of here, the first town to have a coal mine with electric lights. Now Landrus is identified by a stone marker and a few old foundations by the side of a forestry road. Though farms and houses dot the landscape, my tendency to see Tioga County as a wild place has been ingrained through many hours immersed in texts telling me to look for wildness everywhere.

What does this have to do with rhetoric? Plenty, and I didn't realize how I was processing so much about rhetoric until moments like seeing a scarlet tanager started piling up. A group of us were riding one Sunday morning, and we stopped at the spring outside Arnot to refill our water bottles. I was standing with several other cyclists around the PVC pipe where water poured from the spring. We were chatting about how slow we climbed the last hill and how strong one of the local fast guys, Jared, was riding—

typical cyclist talk. As we talked, I scanned the trees, behavior sharpened from time spent with Daddy and reading books by people who spent their time scanning the trees, the deserts, the mountains, the migration routes of ospreys. I look around all the time, because I hope to see something cool. That day I saw the scarlet tanager, which I immediately pointed out to my buds. Sure, the encounter was partly luck, but I also had to be looking for it. Few of my cycling friends see the birds I see on rides, because they don't look for them. Nothing wrong with that. We see nature differently. My habit of paying attention, of looking outside the lines, grows largely out of reading others who paid attention to their surroundings. My attitude toward the awesomeness of nature inclines me to do that, much like a curve in the road impels me to steer my bike in a certain direction.

Which gets us back to rhetoric. Whether on the truck or on my bike, I experience a small slice of physical reality that is mediated by the language, the symbols, I've encountered at home, at school, at work, on the news, wherever via whatever media. The scarlet tanager was real, but I only knew what it was because I had seen them in bird books. In other words, I saw it first as a picture and words on a page, that is, as a representation or symbol of the real thing. In one sense, I was looking for it because I was primed to look closely at nature for those kinds of encounters.

Put another way, we never come to anything as a blank slate. Our understanding and interpretation of any situation is always mediated in some way by language. This is the world we pedal in, a world mostly explained by and understood through symbols. Yes, I said mostly. We are physical critters, but without our symbols, we wouldn't know jack.

Kenneth Burke claims that using symbols is what defines us as human. He writes:

The "symbol-using animal," yes, obviously. But can we
bring ourselves to realize just what that formula implies,
just how overwhelmingly much of what we mean by
"reality" has been built up for us through nothing but our
symbol systems? Take away our books, and what little do we
know about history, biography, even something so "down to
earth" as the relative position of seas and continents? What
is our "reality" for today (beyond the paper-thin line of our
own particular lives) but all this clutter of symbols about
the past combined with whatever things we know mainly
through maps, magazines, newspapers, and the like about
the present? In school, as they go from class to class, students turn from one idiom to another. The various courses
in the curriculum are in effect but so many different ter-
minologies. And however important to us is the tiny sliver
of reality each of us has experienced firsthand, the whole
overall "picture" is but a construct of our symbol systems.
To meditate on this fact until one sees its full implications is
much like peering over the edge of things into an ultimate
abyss. And doubtless that's one reason why, though man is
typically the symbol-using animal, he clings to a naïve verbal realism that refuses to realize the full extent of the role
played by symbolicity in his notions of reality. (1966, 5)

What strikes me about Burke's insight into how much of what
we know is symbolic knowledge is in parentheses: "(beyond the
paper-thin line of our own particular lives)." I go for a bike ride,
and I see a lot. But I don't really begin to understand what I've
seen and where I've been until I read about it in books or look at
maps.

When I share Burke's passage with composition students at the
beginning of a semester, I always ask them what Burke means by

the parenthetical phrase. The answer, of course, is found in the rest of the paragraph—we know what we know because of books and other texts, that is, symbolic knowledge—an idea a few students grasp right away. But many don't. So I ask how many have been to Antarctica. No one raises a hand. Russia? Nothing. North Dakota? Maybe one or two hands go up.

"Then how do we know these places exist?"

"We see pictures on the Internet," some say. Others say, "We saw it on a map."

"Is the net the place itself?" I ask. "Is the map?"

"No."

Then we begin unpacking the idea that we would know very little about the world if we relied on physical experience as the sole source of knowledge.

I see the same issue at work when I look at a map of Tioga County.[5] I spend a lot of time with a map of the county looking at all the roads I've ridden. I've ridden a bunch of them, and I feel like I physically know the county pretty well. But there are still huge swaths I don't know, and I can only see so far from each road I ride. And the map doesn't show whether I'm riding past farms, houses, forests (except state forests), businesses, and so on. The map doesn't tell me the best place to see deer or grouse or where I'm likely to see a bear. I have to learn where those animals might be in other ways. Likewise, I often come back from rides and dig into books to try to figure out whether I saw a sharp-shinned hawk or a Cooper's hawk, whether the leaves I picked up are elm or beech. So even though I have been "down to earth" in my explorations of the county by bike, much of what I know about it comes from symbols.

This gets us to the core issue of being symbol-using animals. Symbols are, at best, inexact representations of the things represented. I look at the Tioga County map, see all the green blocks that demarcate state forests, see the lack of big cities, and say to myself, "That looks like a wild, rural place, because there's not many people there. Cool!" For me, fewer people is good, right up there with "rural" and "wild," which means I see the map representing something I desire or value. But I know people who would look at that map and find it scary for the "lack" of civilization it represents. They see the county as undesirable, a blank space. My urban-dwelling students sum it up: "There's nothing to do around here." Neither of our responses are wrong, but each emphasizes something (wild versus civilized; rural versus urban) that the other does not. The lesson? Symbols can be understood in different ways, depending on what the person reading the symbol brings to his or her reading of it. That also means that symbols can be used in different ways to achieve different ends. When I talk to people about how much I love this place, I emphasize the lack of civilization shown on the map as a strength or feature. "This place is awesome! There's nobody here!" My students who see this place differently, however, tell their friends, "This place sucks! There's nobody here!" Same map, different attitudes. That's how symbols work, whether visual or textual. Put another way, symbols are sloppy. I couldn't say that "bicycle" really means "car"—words aren't that sloppy—but symbols do offer room for multiple readings or interpretations. When people hear the word "bicycle," some think of the cheap steel Huffy they rode as a child; some think expensive, carbon fiber Specialized racing bicycles (that'd be me); some think freedom; some think physical fitness; some think nuisance; some think kid's toy. Everyone knows what a bike is, but the way they define it differs. The use of symbolic language becomes even more complicated when we begin using more abstract words like "jobs" or "patriotism" or "safe." People (or industries) often use symbols in ways that favor the person (or industry) sharing them. It turns out the gas industry is a master of using symbols this way, which we'll explore in more depth later, after I finish telling the story of drilling down my own roots.

—o—

You could say I'm inscribing my own story onto the landscape of Tioga County. When I write, "I saw a scarlet tanager at the spring on Arnot Road," I'm telling a story about the place that puts me in a particular part of it at a particular time, but I'm also writing the larger story of how I got to know this place. I'm telling two stories really, one about a specific bird at a specific spring and one that feeds a larger story about how encounters with wildlife shape my perceptions of this place and connect me. Another story that feeds my overarching narrative involves food.

Before I moved to Pennsylvania, most of my food came from the grocery store, except when, as a kid, I ate out of my parents' and grandparents' gardens. After I left home, that kind of eating was limited to holidays, family reunions, and other visits. In Nevada, Lilace and I bought lamb and beef from a local rancher when we could, which wasn't often. For Thanksgiving, we went in with friends on a free-range turkey from Whole Foods. But mostly our meat came shrink-wrapped in Styrofoam trays. We could have quit eating meat, which we'd done before, but we didn't. We liked meat too much, and, though our attitudes were evolving, they had not shifted enough for us to break up with the industrial food chain.

I wanted out of the Styrofoam food chain because of Richard Nelson. When I was in grad school at WCU, Lilace arranged for Nelson to give some lectures about hunting at WCU and Warren Wilson College. Since we knew him from a nature writing class we had taken in Alaska, part of the deal was that he crash in our spare bedroom. After his talks, we'd sit on the front porch of our trailer across the road from Caney Fork Creek, snacking on deer jerky he had made, while I pestered him about his writing and his ideas on eating and nature. Nels told me that, wherever he travels, he carries homemade deer jerky so he can eat a piece each day to remind himself of his connection to his local food chain. Nels' books, our conversations, and those plastic bags of jerky pushed me to think deeply about what it's like to kill an animal and the need for death to sustain life. I kicked many questions around in my head after his visit. *Shouldn't I be willing to kill what I eat? Can I kill an animal? How will I react? Will it taste different? Is killing an animal I eat really more ethical?* I liked the idea of learning on some level the work many people do to feed others. Mostly, though, I wanted to learn what it was like to be intimate with the so-called "circle of life." I wondered whether I'd have the nerve to make my role in that circle explicit, not just academic. These thoughts nagged me through six more years of grad school.

When I moved to Mansfield, the chance to participate in the circle of life came in the form of a wiry man with unruly black hair and a mustache to match. Mike Chester teaches physics at MU and farms in his spare time. He and his wife own Always Somethin' Farm, about two miles northeast of the university. He raises Heritage turkeys, Cornish Rock chickens, goats, and the occasional pig. He grows wicked good garlic, asparagus, tomatoes, radishes, and raspberries. His Mortgage Lifter tomatoes are my all-time favorites, gnarly beasts growing to the size of a child's plastic bowling ball. His wife makes soap, as well as fabulous sticky buns (great for hangovers), and they homeschooled their daughters, now both in college.

Lilace and I had been living in Mansfield for over a year when we learned we could get our Thanksgiving turkey from Mike. Buying from him appealed to us more than buying a free-range turkey from Wegman's grocery store. When we asked what we needed to do to get on his list, he said, "You're on it." I asked if I could help him butcher.

"Process," he replied, "I call it 'processing.' Yeah, you can help."

"You realize I might show up and chicken out, right?"

"That's fine," Mike said. "My daughter will be happy she doesn't have to help."

I was excited at the prospect of participating in a ritual that I had thought about for years, and nervous. What if I couldn't "process" a turkey? No matter what, at least I'd come face to face with Nelson's idea of food as a gift, even though I wouldn't be hunting. The way I saw it, theory must become practice. Or, in rhetoric's terms, my incipient attitude was about to become physical action. I would test the power of words.

—◦—

The Monday before Thanksgiving, gray morning skies spat snow while wind shook the trees. At 6:45 a.m., I walked out of the driveway into the flurries and turned right toward Mike's farm on Newtown Hill Road, a road that climbed east out of Mansfield toward Highway 549 and a popular route for cyclists. I passed MU's Brooks Maintenance building, the university's water treatment plant, crossed Corey Creek, and followed the road up the hill past a few houses and a small apartment building. A quarter mile later, I crossed a small bridge and bore left onto Mike's gravel driveway. I passed multiflora rose overhanging the drive as I made my way up to the white farmhouse with the red barn out back. Their retriever, Allie, barked at me, and a couple of minutes later, Mike emerged from the house. He wore yellow slickers over his jeans, a Carhartt coat over his sweatshirt, and a fur-lined bomber hat. "Gonna be a cold one," he said.

"Yep," I replied, dropping my pack and pulling out more layers to add to my two cotton shirts, fleece jacket, and water-resistant climbing pants. Boots rounded out our ensembles—for Mike, tall, insulated rubber boots; for me, Gore-Tex-lined hiking boots.

Mike pointed to the barn and said, "We'll be up there. If you want a scone, Chris has some inside."

I popped inside, said hello, and grabbed a scone. Their oldest daughter thanked me for helping her Dad so she didn't have to. I told her I hadn't done anything yet. She shrugged and said, "At least you're here." She'd thank me several more times before the day was over.

The temperature hovered in the thirties and an inch of snow covered the ground when I walked to the barn around 7:30. A small enclosed trailer hitched to a Kubota tractor sat on the right. On the left, a line of coolers sat on parallel 2×4s. At one end stood a clean trash can full of ice water. Behind the trailer rested a cage-looking structure with four aluminum cones nailed to each end. To the left of the structure, a trash can full of hot water sat on concrete blocks while a propane burner hissed underneath it. Just outside the barn, half a blue plastic barrel containing black rubber knobs and attached to a small motor rested in a white 2×4 frame—the plucker, Mike informed me. Beside the plucker, a plywood table with a cutting board and knife. Mike told me that we would eviscerate the turkeys inside the little white cinder-block building beside the coolers where the radio played the local rock station.

"Let's go see the turkeys," Mike said, and I followed him up the hill past the barn to a small coop. Inside, twenty-six heritage Midget White turkeys and four Delaware chickens clucked softly. They seemed calm for birds destined for the block, but what did I know. Mike explained the process to me. I'd follow him up to the shed and make sure no turkeys escaped while he grabbed one. We'd wire the bird's feet together and place its head through a hole drilled in the bottom of a five-gallon bucket. The hole was against the edge of the bucket, I soon learned, so that Mike could pull the turkey's head out flat against a sheet of plywood and decapitate it. We'd hang the turkey a few minutes to bleed, dunk it in the hot water for about forty-five seconds, and run it through the plucker. "Be sure to keep your mouth closed when you're dunking the bird," Mike warned. "You don't want that water to splash into your mouth." He explained that we would remove the legs at the joint before we plucked it, and, post-pluck, drop the bird in the trash can full of ice water. Mike said, "I'll show you the rest when we get all the birds plucked. There's a lot of learning on the job here." I nodded. I had listened carefully and felt the same attentiveness I experienced whenever lining up for a bike race or putting on my tool belt at a job site. Abstractions fall away and I focus on the task at hand, absorbing small bits of data that help me work more carefully and efficiently. I didn't want to be in the way, a fear from my time working construction, nor did I want to set the birds free. Thanksgiving was three days away, and I didn't want to be blamed for twenty families' dinners running loose. I still wasn't sure I'd be able to kill one, but hearing the process explained reassured me that I wouldn't run away either.

The sun broke briefly through the clouds, highlighting the trees west of us with alpenglow, something I used to see out west. "Wow," I said. "Look at that." We admired the gold-tinted trunks a moment. Then Mike said, "Tailgate rules apply. You want a beer?"

"Yeah."

He walked into the barn and emerged with two tallboy Pabsts, Mike's sacramental drink for processing. "We won't have to worry about these getting warm," he said. We opened our beers and took a swig. "Let's go."

We walked back to the shed. Mike entered carefully, and I held the door closed behind him. He grabbed a turkey from among the now not-so-calm birds and said "Okay." I let him out, eyeing the other birds and closing the door quickly. Though worried that I might be in the way or free the birds, I realized I hadn't been thinking about the physical act of killing, an act I had spent hours thinking about over the past several years. Farming is not like hunting. I didn't have to wait for game to show; it was hanging upside down in Mike's hand. I would see death, whether I wanted to or not.

I wired the bird's feet together, and Mike carried it to the cage-like structure that, I learned, was an unused pig crate. Mike had nailed a rectangle of particle board on it with 2×4s nailed down the long sides. A piece of bailing twine was tied across the space between the 2×4s and left with enough slack to allow the five-gallon bucket lying on its side to slip underneath. The contraption held the bucket stable. Mike slid the turkey into the bucket and pulled its head through the hole drilled in the bottom against the edge. He stretched the turkey's neck out on the particle board. Holding the turkey's head firmly in his left hand, he picked up a cleaver and said, "Thank you, bird." He bore down on the turkey's neck with the cleaver, sawed back and forth a couple of times, and cut off its head. The decapitation was quick but not neat—blood spurted from the jugular onto the snow and the back of Mike's old Ford. The headless bird thrashed as Mike hung it upside down to bleed it, its feet scratching furiously against the plastic bucket. Mike showed me the steps one more time before I "processed" a bird.

I became intimate with the chopping block after that. Recalling my conversations with Nelson before bearing down with the cleaver, I looked each bird in the eye and said, "Thanks, Buddy." A little hokey, perhaps, but I appreciated what the bird was giving to me in ways I hadn't before, the blood hot in the cold morning air. It took more effort to cut off the bird's head than I expected, but I focused on doing the job quickly and well, knowing that meant the least amount of suffering.

While blood dripped from the hanging buckets into plastic dishpans, we began to pluck the birds. First, Mike showed me how to slosh the bird up and down in hot water to loosen the feathers. My shoulder strained under the burden of fourteen-pound Midget White held at arm's length and weighted down by water for forty-five seconds. Every so often, I dunked too deep and scalded my fingers. I never cursed aloud though. Keep your mouth closed, remember? Over the course of the day, the water mingled with dust and shit and turned a rich brown. I imagined it would grow good vegetables, but I did not want that water to splash in my face.

After dunking the bird, I lugged it to the plucker and Mike showed me how to cut off the feet. Spraying the carcass with a hose, I flipped on the plucker and watched the blue plastic drum spin the bird clean of feathers. The bird flopped crazily on the knobs, and I was sure it would be damaged in some way. But Mike said the skin would not tear as long as the water did not rise above 67 degrees Celsius and I didn't leave the bird in hot water or the plucker too long. I dropped the plucked bird into the clean trash can filled with ice water. Soon we established a rhythm of processing: decapitating the birds, letting the blood drain, dunking, plucking, and swigging occasionally from a PBR.

After all the birds were killed and plucked, Mike and I shifted our operation into the small cinder-block hut where I prepped the birds for gutting by cutting the scent gland off the tail, plucking any remaining feathers, and loosening the esophagus, a tricky operation that involved running my fingers under the skin along the neck and separating the crop from the skin. It took me several birds to get the feel for what I was doing. Mike eviscerated the birds, taking care to keep the entrails intact so the cavity remained clean. By now it was afternoon, and, though fortified by several more PBRs, we worked quickly to stave off the cold. But we had been wet for several hours, the temp hadn't climbed much, and working barehanded with cold turkey carcasses meant that getting cold was inevitable.

We packed the last turkey in an ice-filled cooler around 3 p.m. We sipped on a couple more PBRs, chatted about the university, and thought of ways we could speed up the processing. My shoulders ached from holding ten- to fourteen-pound birds at arm's length all day while dunking them. My fingers were prunes, my pants were blood-spattered, and feathers and bits of viscera stuck to my boots. I looked and felt like I had done a day's work, and I had "processed" the turkey we were going to eat for Thanksgiving. I looked forward to it, and I knew that, no matter what, I would think it was the best turkey I had ever eaten. Such is the power of participating in the circle of life.

We finished our beers, and Mike drove me home. I stripped off my wet boots and clothes and took a long, hot shower that did not warm me up. I dried off quickly afterward and piled on the clothes. Along with my shoulders, my lower back ached, my hands were sore, and I felt chilled for several hours. I wasn't shivering, just cold to my core. I grabbed another beer, sat on the couch, and stared at the wall, thinking back over the day. I was satisfied with my effort and surprised by the hard work required to feed people. One turkey would have been work; twenty-six (plus four chickens) was more. I was content, even a little proud, that I was able to kill the turkey that would grace my table on Thanksgiving. The turkey lived a humane life and it died humanely, less than two miles from my house. That meant a lot to me. I guessed Nelson would be proud.

To keep alive my sense of connection to my food (poultry, anyway), I've committed to help Mike any time he processes poultry. If he's processing chickens, I drop everything to help. One summer my longtime climbing and cycling compadre John Derry visited from North Carolina, and I dragged him out to the farm to help Mike process fifty Cornish Rocks. John didn't know that would be a part of his vacation. But he took it in stride since it included beer. Once the fifty were packed in ice in coolers, ready to be bagged and weighed, John and I bagged two, took them to the house, rubbed them with butter and herbs, and slow roasted them on the grill. They were superb, seasoned by hard work and Tioga County. Now, whenever Mike and I process birds, we wish John was there to help.

All those words I'd read and heard were made real.

—o—

There are other ways I connect with the county. I teach students from around here, and many share their stories. I hang out around fire rings drinking bourbon and beer with people who grew up here. Riding my bike, eating local food, hearing locals' stories, and telling my own stories connect me to this place in the same way the oak trees in my yard bury their roots. My actions and words mingle with others and create what rhetoricians call a "context," or a web of words and lived experience that help me understand where I am and how I belong. This place is no longer a blank space to me, no longer a Tioga map of pink and purple lines crossing white and green blocks, but a map filled in with memories and experiences. Over the first three years I lived here, I developed, to use that old cliché, a sense of this place.

That changed in 2009 when the gas industry rolled in.

3   The Middle Finger of Progress

⌗   Though it bothered me, I could see benefits of the gas boom. As gas guys filled the rentals on our street, our street got quieter. The spike in rents pushed out the college students, and after working twelve-hour shifts, the gas workers tended to drink a couple of beers and go to bed. The lack of partying college students became part of my argument against moving to the country—"It's quieter, honey!"—but Lilace wasn't buying. And in those moments when I was being honest with myself, I could imagine being a country mouse. I was tired of the noise and seeing the cedar waxwings on the tree outside my office window silhouetted against the house 30 feet away. I wanted my son Gabe to be able to stretch his legs and his imagination a bit. Hell, I wanted to stretch mine. But the uncertainty I felt about the industry intruded on those fantasies like a broken spoke during a bike ride.

When I first heard the phrase "sacrifice zone," I thought it was a bit hyperbolic. At the time, we lived in Mansfield, and the people I heard say it I considered a bit extreme. But my research and my bike rides around the county impressed upon me that the phrase was accurate. I rode past the well pads in all directions and watched as a number of gas companies opened businesses, often in trucking. The county began to remind me of the industrial parks where Daddy delivered freight, though the park I rode my bike through wasn't clustered in some grimy section of Newark or Peoria but spread out over people's backyards and the Commonwealth's state game lands. I heard "sacrifice zone" more often, and I was bothered. No one wants to live in a sacrifice zone.

When I saw a friend post about living in a sacrifice zone on Facebook, I asked her where she heard the phrase. She directed me to Hannah Adelbeck's (2010) "The Risks of Marcellus Shale Drilling Are Worth the Potential Gains, Says PSU Prof," an interview with Penn State professor of geosciences Terry Engelder. Though I had to give him props for being honest, what I read made me angry. *What the hell was this guy thinking?*

Adelbeck summed up Engelder's view, writing that the "environmental risks related to drilling for gas in the Marcellus are worth the costs." Adelbeck noted how Engelder "believes shale gas is the 'simultaneous solution' to five big national problems: huge federal debts and state deficits, an unfavorable balance in international trade, uncomfortably high rates of unemployment, multiple global wars driven in part by perceived threats to supplies of foreign oil, and an uncertain future associated with global climate change." Shale gas sounded promising so far, and many people liked his message. But Engelder's statements began to grate when he brought up sacrifice zones.

Engelder offered a Dark Ages–lite suggestion that the people who question the gas industry want to live in the Dark Ages before moving into the idea that Pennsylvanians must make sacrifices. Adelbeck reported:

> "We all enjoy our lifestyle that we have. 100 trillion cubic feet is responsible for all this," [Engelder] said. "My assumption is that modern man will want to move about the way we do today," he said, adding that he believes our taste for a variety of tropical produce and our enjoyment of light after dark, indoor heat and air conditioning mean that our demand for fossil fuels will not change much.
>
> Engelder said he believes Pennsylvanians must sacrifice to maintain their lifestyle. "My heart goes out to landowners whose mineral rights have been severed," he said. "It's

that type of sacrifice that we're talking about. It's a necessary sacrifice."

Adelbeck noted that Engelder "hope[d]" drillers would "recognize" the residents' sacrifice and called for stringent regulation. But he also recognized the risk, noting that "this is a very complex industry and there will be accidents. . . . People expect that level of risk in automobiles."

Needless to say, Engelder's words pissed me off. Here was a man who had calculated that the Marcellus shale contained close to a trillion cubic feet of gas, spread his number throughout the public sphere, and suggested that shale gas was a "simultaneous solution" to five problems facing America while claiming just a few paragraphs later that he was not an expert in the economics of natural gas. Perhaps the most breathtaking aspect of Engelder's choice of words was what "sacrifice" suggested about how he saw a place where people lived. People carved out homes for themselves here. Sure, some people would profit from the gas industry, but some would lose their homes. Some would do both. Engelder's frame flabbergasted me, and I found it hard to believe that someone tied to the industry the way he was would presume to make that kind of judgment about a place where people lived. My sense that we were relatively safe in town intensified. *What if they trashed our property? We would have nothing. But, hey, at least we could say we took one for the team.*

I had read plenty about other parts of the country being sacrificed at the altar of the fossil fuel and other industries. I saw photos of mountaintop coal mining, read about the chemical industry in the Texas Gulf Coast, and followed the BP disaster in the Gulf and the chemical spill in Charleston, West Virginia. I knew these "sacrifices" happened—more often called "accidents"—and they always happened somewhere other than where I lived. But here was Engelder defining Tioga County as a "sacrifice zone" in the early stages of the gas play. That changed everything. I did not like the idea of Tioga County being seen as somewhere to sacrifice. I was raising my kids here. I wanted more of a say.

Turns out I wasn't the only one.

—o—

My reservations about moving to the country cracked one day when we met our real estate agent at a log cabin off Carpenter Road. I had pedaled by the short, dead-end roads on the south side of Carpenter too many times to count but never wondered much about them. I was drawn to the state game lands on the north side of Carpenter, where I rode my bike, hiked, or picnicked with Lilace and the kids. The cabin stood a few hundred yards away from the bottom of Brown Run Road, a gated forestry road that I often descended after climbing Firetower Road.

The cabin fit our outdoor aesthetic but needed work to complete the kids' bedroom, the tongue-and-groove ceiling over the back porch, and the pole barn out back. The finished rooms wowed us— high ceilings, a cozy living room with a fireplace, sliding glass doors opening onto a big deck, and lots of trees between the cabin and the neighbors' houses. I imagined watching snow dumping outside while a fire popped in the fireplace. The lot was about two acres, there was a sunny garden space out front, and gas rights stayed with the house. Becoming a country mouse suddenly contained possibilities. Fewer people. More space. More quiet. Quicker access to wilder terrain. My soul opened at the thought of it. We had not lived in the country since grad school in North Carolina eleven years earlier. The idea of country life attracted me and began tilting the scales away from my worries about the gas industry.

We put in an offer on the cabin, insultingly low it turned out, because I was worried about the work that needed to be done. But seeing the possibilities suggested by that house began to outweigh my worries about natural gas development. We'd have to keep looking, and be sure to find a house on unleased property—leased property was still a deal breaker—but I could now see making the move. I wasn't less worried, but something about where that cabin sat shifted my attitude enough that moving to the country entered the realm of possibility. I still shared my concerns with Lilace, but without the same heat.

After two years of looking, one failed purchase, and too many arguments to count, in summer 2010 we bought a beautiful, 1860s-era brick Victorian on seven acres of unleased land about seven miles west of Mansfield in Whitneyville, home of the Tioga County Fairgrounds. On Halloween weekend, we moved into what locals called the Whitney house. We traded the noise of drunken college kids for birds singing, roosters crowing, the crack of deer rifles being sighted in, and tractors mowing or hauling hay. Great horned owls hooted insistently in the winter, coyotes yipped along the ridge west of us, and, our first spring, an American woodcock used the grassy acreage beside us as the stage for his sky dance. We heard sand, dump, and water trucks grinding by on Charleston Road about half a mile away as the crow flies, on their way to feed the industry spread around us.

I was happy we moved, the kids were stoked for the yard and the bus ride to school, and Lilace soon had chickens, a garden, and a writing tent pitched in the field behind our house—what our daughter called "Mama's fort." We had rabbits, deer, turkeys, and the occasional bear. Flickers chattered at each other, chickadees nested in a willow east of the house, and red-tail hawks surfed the winds, peeling off the low ridge that marked the back of our property. The brightness of the stars blew my mind when I walked outside at night to piss. On those evenings when there was a Boston butt on the smoker, a fire in the fire ring, kids with sticks running wild in the fields, bourbon in my glass, and friends to share it with under those stars, I was more content than ever before. The country was peaceful in a way the town wasn't. My soul expanded to meet the wildness spread out around me.

My fear and anger bubbled up like flowback whenever I read an article about the possibility of forced pooling or how so-and-so's farm was polluted, though Lilace helped me understand that day-to-day peace of mind, which we had at the Whitney house, was a form of long-term security as necessary as financial security. I've always believed that getting outside (the wilder, the better) is necessary to mental well-being. Whitneyville may not be the Sierra Nevada, but it's the only place I have lived where bears have visited my house.

One problem I wrestled with before we moved to the country was the fact that our move would mean we were supporting an industry we questioned—the place required more fossil fuel energy for us to maintain. Well, less for the house—we downsized by nearly a 1,000 square feet—but more for mowing the yard and driving into town for work, groceries, swim practice, and the like. I haven't done the math, but we ramped up our actions to help us draw less from the fossil fuel hose. We traded in our Toyota Sienna for a Toyota Corolla. Lilace started to grow some of our food, I processed chickens with Mike, and we bought locally as much as possible. We send trash to the landfill once every two or three weeks. I ride my bike to and from work in single-digit temperatures in the winter. It's uphill both ways. Seriously. We've decided that it matters to live close to what we are fighting for—a healthier planet with some wildness left on it. We buried our roots in this place in part through that wildness, rooting in ways that helped us see our place and planet as more than abstractions. The problem with the industry was that it measured its connection to the land in terms of cubic feet per day. Could we drill down roots deeper than the industry?

—◦—

Agents are people who have something to say and who shape messages in particular ways for particular contexts and particular reasons. Rhetoric always involves an agent. We are all agents, and we can examine an agent's rhetorical act to acquire some sense of the agent's attitude toward a subject. My own writing provides an example. My master's thesis focused on images of wildness in Alfred, Lord Tennyson's *Idylls of the King*, his epic poem about the legend of King Arthur. I could just as easily have written about how Guinevere's character represented the oppression of women in Victorian England. Exploring representations of the oppression of women in literature is an important idea, and we have learned a lot from scholars who have pursued such research. But that subject was not my main research interest at the time. I focused on environmental issues instead.[1] The book you hold in your hands focuses on how rhetoric used by extractive industries influences the way we see and use places. Its *raison d'etre* is my concern about nature, climate change, and the effects of industry rhetoric on how we see and use places. We need to care for the world we live in, and we owe it to ourselves and the land to understand how the rhetoric we craft and encounter shapes our attitudes toward it.

As we were looking at houses, the industry told us one story about gas. Academics told us another. Politicians told us another. Activists told us another. Friends told us yet another. When we moved to the country, we lived in the midst of a large, ongoing, multimedia conversation between the industry, government officials, lobbyists, environmental groups, and the people who lived over the shale. These agents shaped their messages in ways that suited their goals, whether those goals were profit, jobs and economic growth, energy independence, protecting the environment, or something else. The messages overlapped one another and came in the form of websites, press releases, TV, radio, and print advertisements, letters, contracts, phone messages, billboards and signs, news coverage, blogs, art (quilts, photography, pottery, and pastel landscapes, to name a few), bumper stickers, protests, books, bills, policy statements, scientific research, Google groups, and public meetings. The flurry of words flew around the county like a February snow.

All of these words bandied about on developing the Marcellus shale created what Marilyn Cooper called a "web" of language (1986, 370), a web that supplied much of what I knew about the industry and how it connected to the geography of this place. The web evolved over time, stretching, deforming, and reforming into new shapes and relations as each agent shared a rhetorical act and tried to nudge attitudes toward whatever condition (unfettered access to gas, untrammeled public land, uninterrupted quiet at home) the industry, politicians, environmentalists, or the public desired.[2]

Like everyone living in Tioga County, we found ourselves enmeshed in a cacophony of voices and messages that offered competing ideas about developing the resource of natural gas. Burke characterized such situations as "the Scramble, the Wrangle of the Market Place, the flurries and flare-ups of the Human Barnyard" (1950, 20–3).[3] The barnyard is Burke's metaphor for situations in which a number of different voices clamor for different things with different goals and desires in mind. Like all barnyards, some voices are louder than others.

Millions of words had been written about the Marcellus shale by the time Lilace and I bought the Whitney house. The State Library of Pennsylvania databases tell an interesting tale about when those words appeared in print. The ABI/INFORM Trade and Industry database suggests the industry's interest in the Marcellus shale preceded the public's, which gave the industry an advantage in framing the message we heard about developing the natural gas resource. The industry had nearly four years to think and talk about its plans for drilling before the press began informing the public at comparable levels.[4] Absent any dissenting voice from outside the industry questioning what authors wrote about the shale in the trade publications, the articles served as a kind of echo chamber, reinforcing their attitudes toward the shale play. Because members of the industry were talking to each other, instead of the people who lived above the shale, their early messages to the public suggested they saw this place as worth something only in terms of the gas trapped in the ground. It's as if the barnyard they lived in was overrun with one type of animal—say, asses—and their braying drowned out everything else.

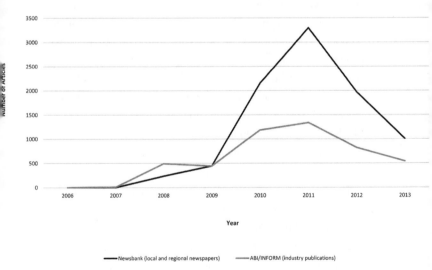

Publication of "Marcellus Shale" Articles

Comparison of Marcellus Shale coverage in industry publications and local and regional newspapers. Graph by Sheila Kasperek

When we heard them, the industry's messages were positive. Natural gas promised to become a bridge fuel to alternative energy sources, a means of national energy independence, and an economic boon to the county, state, and country. While the industry provided the same basic message regardless of the context, locals encountered articles, reports, and stories from neighbors and friends that fractured the industry's prevailing narrative. I read that a woman's water well exploded in Dimock, Pennsylvania, and radioactive material had been discovered in flowback water. In 2010 and 2011 there were so many news articles and reports full of new terminology coming out that I felt overwhelmed, like the character in the film *Brazil* who disappears under a swirl of papers. Between family and teaching obligations, I simply couldn't read them all, which left me feeling underinformed.

Dimock was one example of what was happening at the time. While Lilace and I were still in prepurchase arguments, I read about Dimock, a township about two hours east of Mansfield. Dimock became known for thirteen water wells being contaminated by methane due to faulty gas wells drilled by Cabot Oil and Gas Corporation. I first heard the news from my colleague, Kristin Sanner, who lived near Dimock. After talking to Kristin, I researched the story and saw some of my worst fears realized. Abrahm Lustgarten (2009) of ProPublica reported that Dimock resident Norma Fiorentino's water well exploded due to a build-up of methane. Lustgarten then reported that research in Ohio and Colorado suggested that gas drilling may have more of an impact on water wells than originally suspected.

Later in 2009, Laura Legere reported that, after much back and forth between Cabot, the Pennsylvania Department of Environmental Protection, and the homeowners, Cabot would be held responsible for providing "permanent water supplies" to the families whose wells had been affected (2009, A1). Since then, Dimock has become one of the go-to examples (along with DISH, Texas) for illustrating potential problems with the gas industry. The Dimock story revealed how Cabot used stalling tactics to distance itself from responsibility even as it agreed to supply families with water. Legere's story also revealed the Pennsylvania Department of Environmental Protection's and the US Environmental Protection Agency's wishy-washy stances.[5]

Five days after Legere's article hit the newsstands, New York's Binghamton *Press & Sun-Bulletin* led the front page with "State Files Outline Drilling Accidents." Reporter Tom Wilbur summarized the work of Walter Hang, a researcher based in Ithaca and president of Toxic Targeting, a company Hang created to provide environment-oriented research to businesses and government organizations. Wilbur reported that Hang's research uncovered 270 drilling accidents going back to 1979. In response to Hang's research, New York's Department of Environmental Conservation (DEC) pointed out that the number of gas industry accidents was small—"less than 0.1 percent"—compared to the total number of spills listed in the database. Hang responded that his biggest issue with DEC was its assumption that "existing regulations are just fine." Hang argued for tighter regulations, and Wilbur reported that "More than three-quarters of oil and gas problems were caught by somebody other than a DEC staff member." Wilbur also reported that DEC's Linda Collart responded to Hang's research by saying that "We don't anticipate any significant emergencies. . . . These things are rare." Questioned about the state's preparedness for increased drilling activity, Collart stated, "We have been doing fine so far. . . . No problems" (Wilber 2009, 1A, 5A).[6] I struggled to square Collart's words with what happened in Dimock. *How can even a small percentage of problems justify keeping things the same? People are losing their homes.*

New York's DEC had no pull in Pennsylvania, so, technically, Dimock was not New York's issue. But given the lack of oversight in Pennsylvania, Legere's and Wilbur's articles were published before we bought the Whitney house, and they contributed to my unease about buying in the country.[7] Taken collectively, the stories demonstrate how the industry is talked about in an abstract sense when things are going well, like when land is leased or mergers are made, yet when pollution occurs, it happens to specific people in particular places. The rhetoric used by the industry mystifies its relationship with the place it drills. It's not that jobs or lease money are bad, but they are transcendent and apply to any place. Collart's claim that accidents are "rare" downplays consequences for people in places like Dimock by putting those people in an abstract frame based on a small percentage that equals, in Collart's terms, "no problems."

Throughout the gas boom, New York played it safe as a state, much to the chagrin of some New York residents and politicians and the envy of some Pennsylvania residents (me!). New York declared a moratorium on slick-water hydraulic fracturing before the industry rolled in, hoping to learn more about the long-range impacts. I envied their caution and wished Pennsylvania's leaders had it. Since the New York border is only about 20 miles north of Mansfield, Lilace and I briefly kicked around the idea of buying a house there, though higher taxes and the long commute nixed that idea. Instead, we watched New York learn from the grand experiment playing out in the state of Pennsylvania and hoped.

––◦––

One of the most powerful strategies we, as agents, use to shape a persuasive or symbolic message involves identifying ourselves with our audiences. Burke claims that "You persuade a man only insofar as you can talk his language by speech, gesture, tonality, order, image, attitude, idea, *identifying* your way with his" (1950, 55–9). When I head back to North Carolina, my accent intensifies and identifies me as a Southerner, by God. My speech slows and thickens, and I draw out my words, a change that I don't notice until my wife points it out. Since my accent marks me as a Southerner, I don't have to work as hard to get Southern people to listen to me. My accent gives me an "in" because it marks me as a member of the club. In other contexts, however, like at the university, my accent might work against me. A Southern accent implies "redneck" or "inbred, racist, dumb shit" in some contexts, which means I tone my accent down and find other ways to gain the respect and trust of my audience.[8]

We can appeal to audiences in any number of ways, and we must, if we plan to get any of our messages heard. Symbolic acts persuade more effectively when we seek out common ground (or common accents) with people before we try to change (or reinforce) opinions or attitudes. That was one reason industry rhetoric focused heavily on jobs and the economy. The gas industry understood the need for identifying itself with its audience, and it did so in smart ways. (Still does.) After all, the industry was talking to two major audiences—the local one made up of people who live above the Marcellus shale and the national one spread across the United States. A good example was when Louis D'Amico discussed the chemicals in frack fluid in terms of consumer goods and cosmetics, a common industry comparison. D'Amico linked fracking chemicals with what we have under our sinks and in our bathrooms. We identified one with the other. And if we use the same stuff, the chemicals must be safe, right? Of course the public generally doesn't keep thousands of gallons of chemicals in their homes, but D'Amico's goal was to find similarities between people's behaviors and the industry's. Likewise, if we are worried about jobs more than the environment, we are likely to believe that too much taxation and too many regulations will hurt us.

When Lilace and I started blogging about living above the Marcellus shale,[9] part of the motivation for me involved trying to expunge the academic-speak from my writing. I wanted to write about living above the shale in a way that sounded like a chat around a fire or a bullshit session around the bed of a pickup. Not that academic-speak is all bad—I learn a lot from academics—but they (okay, we) can be hard to identify with sometimes because of our language.

My academic background told me that if I was going to make any meaningful changes in how my place was used by the industry, I needed to understand the industry's rhetoric. That's why I read and researched and took a ton of notes. I attended meetings. I asked questions. I rode my bike and weighed the industry's words and images against what I saw happening to the land. My reading revealed patterns in the industry's message that affected how people saw this place (which I talked about in chapter 1).

In 2009 and 2010, the industry's messages resonated powerfully here and across the nation, a power achieved by making the place where I drilled down roots seem abstract, a blank space on the map. This was nothing new for extractive industries, and it identified us with our history. I saw in the industry's desire to drill the desires of the Puritans to carve out a life in the New World or of the settlers who tamed the West during Manifest Destiny. Even though Native Americans lived in America during both periods, the outsiders saw the land as a blank space waiting to be conquered, inhabitants be damned. Though we are more enlightened now, we are also products of that kind of thinking. The industry understood our collective history, and it shaped its messages to focus attention on the gas itself instead of the people living over the shale.

The industry created the impression that Tioga County was abstract space in part by drawing on our shared history of westward expansion to nudge us to look toward the future. Industry rhetoric says "Look toward the horizon, not at the ground under your feet." The industry wanted people to think about Tioga County in ways similar to how our ancestors saw the American West during the nineteenth century—a resource waiting to be seized. People are more likely to accept natural gas drilling when they look at it through the frame of the frontier. The frontier is somewhere else, not in our backyards. Except now it was in mine.

Humanistic geographer Yi-Fu Tuan helps us understand how the industry abstracts a place when he explains the difference between space and place. Tuan writes that "Place is security, space is freedom: we are attached to the one and long for the other" (1977, 1). Tuan characterizes space as "a resource that yields wealth and power when properly exploited. It is a worldwide symbol of prestige. The 'big man' occupies and has access to more space than lesser beings" (58). Tuan's framework helps us see how the industry's framing of northcentral Pennsylvania as a frontier ripe for exploration appealed to the public's collective desire for freedom. This was especially important to the industry's rhetoric directed to the nation. Many of us are not likely to approve of drilling in a place we feel connected to because our memories and lived experiences give such places tremendous value. But if we have no personal connection? We no longer see the area as a place but a space. We're more likely to drill.

Lilace and I experienced the industry's abstracting rhetoric first hand when we moved into the Whitney house. One day, we noticed that the road we now lived on, Orebed Road, had sprouted new signs proclaiming "Pipeline Road 7." The industry added its own signs, signs that suggested little connection to the place. Pipeline Road 7 would work just as well in Texas, Wyoming, Louisiana, or on any other Pennsylvania road.[10] After

I noticed the first Pipeline Road 7 sign, I started seeing pipeline road signs everywhere, especially when I rode my bike. The signs mapped the industry's presence onto the landscape and ignored the connection between the local name and the place itself. The signs prioritized gas, not the place.

The pipeline road signs popping up all over Tioga County signaled one small way that the place was being turned into a blank space on the map. The industry's rhetorical act writ large consisted of more complex "signs" in the form of press releases, advertisements, and op-eds for newspapers. One of the prime movers in this campaign was the Marcellus Shale Coalition (MSC, formerly the Marcellus Shale Committee), a pro-industry trade group that had (and perhaps still has) the loudest pro-gas voice in the region. MSC shaped much of the pro-gas messaging about the gas industry's impacts and attempted to create a perception of the region as a resource instead of a community.

When I checked the MSC website, I found it went right to the business of abstracting the Marcellus shale region. Only 129 words, the mission statement captures concisely the industry's major arguments for why we should develop the Marcellus shale:

The Marcellus Shale: Energy to fuel our future

Welcome to the Marcellus Shale Coalition's (MSC) website. You'll find information on the Marcellus Shale formation, how we extract the natural gas and protect the environment, why we value the communities where we do business, and the opportunities that the Commonwealth and its residents can realize in the coming years and decades through natural gas exploration and production.

You'll also learn about the important issues being addressed by our Marcellus Shale Coalition and the positive impacts natural gas drilling is already having on families, businesses and communities in many parts of Pennsylvania.

So for some quick facts or more in-depth information, we invite you to explore the MSC website and discover why Marcellus Shale is the energy to fuel our future. ("The Marcellus Shale" 2012)

I found MSC's videos and descriptions of gas drilling clear and fascinating—no surprise—and the mission statement raised issues designed to tap into attitudes held by people reading it. Few people want to live in a polluted environment or a fractured community, and many recognize that any type of change like natural gas extraction could possibly lead to one or both of these. MSC attempted to ease these concerns in its mission statement, promising to explain "how we extract the natural gas and protect the environment, why we value the communities where we do business, and the opportunities that the Commonwealth and its residents can realize in the coming years and decades through natural gas exploration and production." Protecting the environment, valuing communities, and providing opportunities suggests that MSC has our deepest concerns at heart, though it is telling that MSC no longer puts the natural gas industry in the subject position ("we") when they discuss opportunities provided by the shale. Readers who encounter the phrases with MSC in the subject position, like "how we provide opportunities that the Commonwealth and its residents can realize in the coming years and decades . . ." or "why we work hard to give the Commonwealth and its residents opportunities to . . ." might hold MSC accountable for what happens during development of the play. MSC obscures itself as an actor, a way to avoid responsibility. When it comes time to talk money, MSC wants people who read the statement to imagine themselves profiting from the industry's work in the future, an especially powerful message in an economically depressed area like Tioga County.

In order for its rhetoric to have any effect, MSC's mission statement must tap into attitudes held to varying degrees by a variety of people living in a variety of circumstances in a variety of geographies spread out over the Marcellus shale. Since the shale band extends under northern and western Pennsylvania across approximately two-thirds of the state, it must craft the rhetoric for rural, suburban, and urban audiences. The shale runs under Washington County, southwest of Pittsburgh, over 200 miles from Tioga County. Washington County has the third highest number of wells drilled in Pennsylvania. It has a population of over 200,000, and most people live within an hour of Pittsburgh, a city of two million. The population of Tioga County checks in around 40,000, and the closest city on Pittsburgh's scale is a four-hour drive away.

I'm sure people who live in Washington County share many of the same concerns raised by the mission statement that I do, but we do not live in the same place. Washington County is an abstraction to me. I have no connection to the place, other than looking at it on a map and reading a Wikipedia entry. I know it's in southwestern Pennsylvania and a lot of drilling occurs there. Because the Marcellus shale runs underneath Washington County and Tioga County, MSC has to create a message that meets the needs of a county containing a denser, suburban and urban population only a few miles outside of Pittsburgh *and* a rural county with one-fifth of the population.

Given the area's proximity to Pittsburgh, people who live in Washington County probably care more about urban and suburban issues than those of us who live in Tioga County. It's not that one group's concerns are more important than another's. Just different. But when we read a statement from MSC that raises issues we identify with, we immediately apply those concerns to our specific circumstances. That's one of the powers of abstractions—they can be imposed onto to all sorts of situations or places, whether or not they reflect those situations or places accurately.

Abstractions tell partial truths. MSC's rhetoric gives the game away when it limits itself to teaching the public about "positive impacts." Everyone appreciates positive change, but few changes on this scale are only positive. MSC's use of "positive" reminds me of the way college administrators toss out the word "excellence." Both words sound good, but once you start trying to define them, they become difficult to pin down. In the industry's case, we saw positive benefits of the gas industry, like good-paying jobs; crowded bars, hotels, and restaurants; and lucrative leases for landowners. They are also only part of the story. We also saw increased traffic, destroyed roads, higher crime rates, paltry gas leases for some, and negative environmental impacts. Some people lost homes or health. Or both. Though MSC wanted the industry to be seen as overwhelmingly "positive," reality is not that neat.

By focusing on the positive, MSC creates the perception of the region as abstract by focusing our attention on the future. When MSC suggests these opportunities will extend "into the coming years and decades," it asks the reader to look to the future. This is Disney princess logic: always look forward to meeting your prince while dismissing any mistreatment in the present.

For instance, MSC's mission statement begins and ends with the phrase "energy to fuel our future." Between 2009 and 2011, politicians, pro-gas newspaper editorialists, industry CEOs, and others proclaimed some version of this phrase in any number of contexts. Responding to protestors outside an industry conference in Philadelphia, Chesapeake Energy CEO Aubrey McClendon stated: "What a glorious vision of the future [the protestors' hold]: It's cold, it's dark and we're all hungry" (Rubinkam 2011, 4A). Speaking about natural gas development at a manufacturing plant visit in Johnstown, Pennsylvania Governor Tom Corbett told a crowd of business owners and politicians "It's not just jobs. [. . .] It's national security. It's national defense. It's a future for our children, our grandchildren" (Siwy 2011). McClendon conjured images of the Dark Ages, of regressing, which contrasted sharply with the warm, bright, comfortable future his words suggest. Corbett raised issues of jobs, safety, and energy independence and ended by suggesting that the development of the Marcellus shale promised a safe future for two generations of children. But when industry rhetoric focuses primarily on the future, it downplays concerns about the present. The present affects children too. By prompting people to imagine possible futures provided by natural gas drilling, the industry directs our attention away from the problems in the present and the past.[11] Metaphorically, the future suggests a sense of progress, of moving forward or up.[12] Such appeals to the future reverberated throughout industry rhetoric and tapped into our deeply held attitudes about the need for progress, echoing the way our Puritan and cowboy ancestors tamed the wilderness. Since the future is, at best, an abstract fiction, MSC presented the messages about the future it thought best aligned with prominent attitudes held by its audience. By doing so, MSC asks people living over the shale to turn their eyes toward fat bank accounts and away from polluted air and water and degraded state forests. Understandably, many did so, because we all hope for a brighter future.

As stated by MSC and later McClendon and Corbett, the gas industry's vision of the future focused heavily on economic development and jobs in order to tap into attitudes people held about work and security. MSC emphasized economic development and jobs at a time when, nationally, we were in a recession, and the economic outlook was bleak. Locally, much of the drilling occurred in rural areas like Tioga County, which had lost manufacturing jobs and financial support for farming.[13] Building on its claim in the mission statement, MSC stated that "The development of natural gas from Marcellus Shale offers great potential for the region's economic future, as well as the thousands of individuals, families, and small, locally owned businesses involved in extracting this clean-burning and abundant energy source from the ground" ("Opportunity" 2012). MSC asked people to think about what could be, not what was, a message that could apply to any shale formation in the United States, just like Pipeline Road 7 would work for any road.

Given what I heard from people who had leased their land or were being pressured to lease, I knew MSC shared partial truths at best, saying in essence, "Look over there!" while the trucks rumbled by in the opposite direction. As MSC's message saturated the county, I heard stories bubble up about polluted property, and I pedaled roads where asphalt had become gravel, varying my bike routes to avoid the damn trucks. Viewed in one way, such activities can be seen as progress; viewed in another, they can be seen as destruction. MSC's rhetoric focused on the former. I found myself divided: happy for friends who had benefited from the industry and scared that the rosy future presented by the industry would resemble the Onceler's in *The Lorax*, after all the truffula trees were chopped down.

—◦—

One thing many people appreciate (or should) when it comes to understanding something or making decisions is data or research— you know: evidence. The MSC recognizes this and includes a link to a study called "An Emerging Giant: Prospects and Economic Impacts of Developing the Marcellus Shale Natural Gas Play" (Considine et al. 2009). Written by faculty associated with Penn State's Marcellus Shale Center for Outreach and Research, the study claimed that "developing these natural gas reserves will directly generate thousands of high-paying jobs and indirectly create many others as employment is stimulated in support industries and as workers spend these wages and households spend royalty income." MSC provided some numbers from the study's projected impacts, like jobs created and dollars generated, and the study bolstered MSC's projections for a rosy future in Tioga and the surrounding counties.

As I looked more closely at MSC's research, I realized it worked inside an echo chamber.[14] I knew that Terry Engelder, the prof who helped ignite the boom, was on the faculty at Penn State (Engelder and Lash 2008). Since Engelder had a dog in this hunt, I decided to dig into Penn State's research. Turns out, when it first came out, the "Emerging Giant" report did not mention that it was funded in part by the MSC, which gave the researchers $100,000. Once this news reached the public, there was much hullabaloo, and the authors were forced to acknowledge that they had received funding from the gas industry, a caveat they included in subsequent reports that could have changed the audience's response.[15]

That MSC farmed out its research to university faculty gave its statements about the future of natural gas development the imprimatur of authority. The report carried the Penn State logo, and it was written to appear disinterested and academic. More telling was the fact that MSC and the Penn State researchers hid the relationship until the Responsible Drilling Alliance and others called them on it. Subsequent reports from the same series state clearly on the second or third page that the reports are funded by MSC and do not necessarily represent the views of Penn State. Seeing those statements changed the way I responded to the report.

Though I wanted to trust MSC and the Penn State researchers and see locals benefit, I had a hard time doing so when the institutions making the projections were talking to themselves. Yet the research supported the promising future MSC wanted people to believe in. That's the problem with using an abstract future to frame actions in the present: such framing enables people with particular interests (the gas industry) to shape their messages in such a way that those messages promote the action (drilling for gas) they want in a way that doesn't account for all the effects. Like I said before, there's nothing surprising about MSC's strategy, but such shenanigans make it difficult for the public to understand clearly the reality of drilling in the Marcellus. This made the ground under the Whitney house seem a little less stable.

Tuan (1977) suggests that the future is a psychological concept similar to abstract space—we project into the future what we want to happen or hope will happen, not necessarily what will happen. MSC tapped into our hopes for a brighter future like the rigs drill into the shale. People who heard positive messages from MSC and politicians about the jobs and the economic boost that would accompany drilling did not connect those impacts directly to physical places. Out of sight, out of mind.

Eventually, the locals' rhetoric vibrated through the natural gas industry's web in ways that pushed the industry to respond. Perhaps the most striking example was Chesapeake Energy's "This Is Our Home" ad campaign. Full-page newspaper ads proclaimed "This Is Our Home" above a picture of a drill rig in the Pennsylvania landscape, followed by text that echoed MSC's message: Chesapeake "take[s] pride in safe, environmentally friendly operations as we create energy security for America, revenue for local communities and jobs for Pennsylvanians." Below the text, the ad displays thirty-six 1.2"×1.3" portraits of individuals who work for Chesapeake, including their names, job titles, and where they presumably live. The ad lends the Oklahoma-based Chesapeake a sense of rootedness in the region and recognizes the company's desire to identify itself with local concerns, something that occurred only after the industry had been around a couple of years. I saw former students in the ads.

—○—

I was sitting at my desk one day, writing. The phone rang. I looked at the screen and saw Daddy's number. I picked up the phone.

"Hello."

"Hey, buddy," Daddy drawled. "How y'all doin'?"

"Fine, I reckon. How's the weather down there?" We compare notes on North Carolina and Pennsylvania weather and catch up on the kids. He turned serious.

"Is that natural gas stuff really as clean as they say it is?"

"Hell, no," I said, thinking, *Marcellus Shale Committee: 1, Tioga County: 0*, before I launched into a description of the trucks, the noise, and the slashing of forests and fields.

4 Gloria's Mountain

⁜ While the gas industry created an image of Tioga County as a blank space on a map, Lilace and I drilled roots into the rocky soil. Our sense of the county was rich and complex, created from, among other things, getting to know people in town, visiting farms and fire rings out of town, hiking the trails in state game lands, and watching three screech owls hanging out above our heads during a backyard barbecue. I rode my bike all over the county, sometimes marveling at—most times disgusted by—the amount of equipment I saw scraping and drilling its way across and into the landscape. I'd pedal by another drill rig on a five-acre pad, middle finger at full extension, a fleet of storage tanks squatting around it like knuckles, trucks rattling by kicking up dust, and I'd wonder: *What the fuck are we doing here*? These images blasted into my good memories of the place.

In 2009, the Friday before Gabe started kindergarten, Lilace and I bought burgers at the Mansfield Grower's Market to celebrate Gabe's milestone. We spent some time at the market almost every Friday, held in the yard of the St. James Episcopal Church. Even with the gas trucks rumbling and creaking by just feet away on Route 6, the market had become the place to be on Friday afternoon. Pop-up tents covered locally grown produce, baked goods, cut flowers and herbs, dairy products, and all kinds of meat. Kids chased each other while adults filled their cloth bags with food for the week or stood in small groups, catching up with friends.

At the time, our house search and arguments were in full swing, though on this evening Lilace and I somehow declared a temporary truce. The sky was clear and a light breeze blew as we gathered our burgers, bags of produce, and the kids and headed for the car for an impromptu picnic in the state game lands on Firetower, a short drive out of Mansfield. As we drove, the smell of burgers mingled with my satisfaction that the cows they came from were raised on a farm about 20 miles west of Mansfield. For me, satisfaction is a powerful spice when it comes to food. Knowing the farmer and the farm adds as much flavor as salt, pepper, and Worchestershire.

The game lands were almost always deserted, except during hunting season, and tonight was no exception. I pulled into the small parking lot near the base of a cellphone tower and parked. Small fields have been carved in the forest north and west of the parking lot, fields usually planted in soybeans to feed the wildlife. Since trees were removed to create the fields, Firetower offers, for the price of a short walk from the parking lot, a fantastic view of Armenia Mountain to the east. Seeing that view explains why this part of the Appalachians is called the Endless Mountains.

I unfolded our bag chairs, set them in the empty parking lot, and opened a couple of Yuengling Lagers while Lilace set the kids up with their burgers. As usual, our son ate his burger without complaint—that boy likes beef—while our daughter squirmed in her little blue chair, claiming not to like hers and begging for a peach. Lilace and I laughed at her and cajoled her into eating three more bites—our mantra every dinner—before she dared eat the peach. The wind rustled the oaks and maples while squirrels and chipmunks crashed around in the underbrush. Cool enough for a sweatshirt but not cold. Protesting to the end, our daughter choked down her three bites and then dug into her peach with three-year-old gusto. Having finished eating long before his sister, our son wandered off to look for "swords" (sticks) and chase chipmunks. Hearing his sister exclaiming about the peach, however, brought him running. Soon, both finished their peaches and wandered off to collect acorns. Given a moment's peace, Lilace and I finished our burgers and beers and discussed our plans for the weekend.

After we cleaned up and put the chairs back in the car, we took the kids on a short hike down Stephenhouse Road, a forestry road that descends the back side of Firetower toward Ives Run Creek four miles away. For fifty or so yards, we followed the Mid-State Trail, which crosses the parking lot before it turns off Stephenhouse and into the woods. We walked past the county's dead animal dumping spot, pointed out to me by a friend while out mountain biking one day. He warned me, "Gotta watch for bears here." No bears this evening. We walked past soybean fields on both sides of the road and into the forest.

Huge oaks towered over the road as it began to drop sharply. If we continued on Stephenhouse to the end, we would end up at Hammond Lake. Too little time and too little light for that tonight. While Lilace and I chatted about the windmills being built on Armenia Mountain, the kids decided to race each other down a steep hill about 200 yards long. Gabriel's graceful six-year-old stride contrasted with Gloria's three-year-old run-waddle. I watched, torn between yelling at them to slow down and cheering them on for the laughter bubbling from their lungs. When the grade flattened, Lilace and I yelled "Stop!" Waiting for us to catch up, the kids climbed on a small boulder. Once we caught up, Lilace pointed out coyote poop in the road, which the kids examined closely. After two more trips across the boulder, we pointed the kids back up the hill toward the car. I expected to carry Gloria, but she put her head down and bulled her way up the hill ahead of us, calling out "This mountain is Gloria's Mountain!" At the top, Lilace and Gabriel walked ahead, while Gloria and I moseyed back to the car, stopping often to squint at flowers and rocks in the gathering dusk. We made it back to the car at dark, and I eased down Firetower Road while the kids and Lilace negotiated which movie we would watch when we got home.

Gloria's words, "This mountain is Gloria's Mountain," marked this place for me, like the gas industry's words do. Though my daughter's words showed that conquering instinct that's found, apparently, in humans of every age, she wasn't extracting anything other than a vague memory of racing her brother down and up a hill one evening after eating a burger and a peach. For me, however, watching my kids on that hill created a different memory, a connection that fed the story I told myself about this place. I was impressed by my kids' ability to run down and climb up that hill, an effort similar to me riding my bike on it, though I never have the wind to laugh. I will never go up or down that hill again without thinking of it as Gloria's Mountain, a name that, unlike Pipeline Road 7, suggests a specific place. A connection, not abstraction or extraction. I spent a peaceful Friday evening with my family in a place that matters to me because I inscribed it with memories and realized the mountains here shape my kids' legs the same way they shape mine. These types of memories give me the sense that I am rooting into the land. Such memories are fertilizer, organic of course, for my carefully cultivated sense of belonging to this place.

Another image: My daughter comes home from a friend's farm, her arms marked with red scratches like she had attacked them with a red pen. The culprit? Kitten claws, a living toy she can't resist trying to pick up, no matter how many times she gets scratched. It bodes well for her mothering instincts. Like my daughter, I don't mind getting scratched, especially if I'm doing something I want to do, like ripping through the barberries crowding the trail at Asaph on my mountain bike. I'm marked, as if taking notes while pedaling through forests I love. Sometimes, though, I wonder if the gas industry scratches my sense of this place too deeply to heal. Or maybe gouges it. Scratches are cosmetic; gouges often require a doctor. Perhaps stitches.

—◦—

We moved in October of 2010. I heard a lot about local gas company East Resources in the months prior to the move. East was a Pennsylvania company at the vanguard of drilling in the Marcellus. While we signed papers to sell our house and buy the Whitney house, I kept hearing that East was in trouble. I couldn't figure out what was going on.

Founded by Penn State grad Terry Pegula and others, East quickly became a major player in developing the Marcellus resource. A small player compared to Shell and Exxon/XTO, East Resources was based in Warrendale, Pennsylvania. In 2009, East "drilled 72 new wells in [Tioga County], and their activities [were] only growing," and by January 13, 2010, East had leased 253,000 acres in the county, or "about 35% of Tioga County's area" and was pursuing more (Przybycien 2010b, 14). The stories I heard and read about East profoundly impacted the way I saw the place.

Reporting on East in the local paper appeared mixed, and in late 2009 and early 2010, reports appeared often.[1] On February 3, 2010, the *Wellsboro Gazette* announced "County Inks East Leases." Jason Przybycien reported that "the Tioga County Board of Commissioners unanimously approved 11 natural gas leases" with East, which gave East subsurface rights "to the gas under 328.23 acres of county properties in Charleston Township. The leases would pay $1,500 per acre totaling $493,245 [and included] a 15 percent royalty for the county on gas extracted [while disallowing] surface drilling and storage on the land" (2010a, 1-A).[2] A month later, the *Wellsboro Gazette* announced that "East Resources Supports Tioga County 4-H with $50,000." Quoting East's executive vice president Bob Long, the article stated, "'East Resources has a major stake in Tioga County's future through its oil and gas interests, and our contribution to this endowment reflects East's commitment to help sustain that future. [. . .] Tioga County's young men and women are the key to the long-term health of our communities, and we appreciate the significant role that the county 4-H program plays in helping them grow into productive, self-directed citizens'" (2010, 1-A). Many other articles touting East's positive impact on the county appeared around this time, projecting a glowing image of the company.[3] But other articles suggested a different story.

On June 20, 2010, the front page of the *Wellsboro Gazette* blurted "State Watches Cows after Frack Spill." Jason Przybycien reported that the "spill occurred when a mixture of fresh water and flowback water seeped out of an impoundment at the Johnson 435 1H well site along Route 362/Pinecreek Road" (2010c, 1-A). Since no one knew whether the cows had eaten or drunk anything contaminated before the spill was cleaned up, the adult cows were quarantined until November 2010. Calves born after the spill were quarantined until January, and calves born before the spill were quarantined for two years. According to East's director of external affairs Stephen Rhoads, East cleaned up the spill to DEP specifications by May 5 (Przybycien 2010c, 1-A). On August 4, 2010, a little over three months before we moved to the Whitney house, the *Wellsboro Gazette* announced, "New Study Tracks Marcellus Shale Drilling Violations." Natalie Kennedy reported that analysis of DEP records by the Pennsylvania Land Trust Association (PLTA) revealed "1,435 violations in 2.5 years" (2010a, 1-A). The PLTA's press release noted that 952 violations could have negative environmental impacts while the remaining violations involved administrative or safety violations. PLTA's report included a list of the top twenty-five violators, and Kennedy reported that East was number one. Kennedy noted, however, that East's average number of violations per well drilled was lower than twenty-one other companies. East's Rhoads blamed the problem on poor erosion and sedimentation practices, incorrect impound-ment construction, and improper pipeline work near streams and wetlands (Kennedy 2010a, 1-A). More articles on the positive and negative impacts of East appeared as we prepared to move to the country. Though I looked forward to getting out of town, that the stories were positive and negative did little to allay my fears. Then I heard another story making the rounds about East that I hadn't seen in the *Gazette*: East was in financial trouble.

Sometime in June 2010, I learned that Royal Dutch Shell was buying East, information that appeared on June 2, 2010, when the *Mansfield Gazette* announced: "Shell Will Buy East Resources." Lacking a byline, the press release stated that East had reached "a definitive agreement to sell the company's principal subsidiaries to an affiliate of Royal Dutch Shell PLC for $4.7 billion." The release noted that "the sale includes East's natural gas and oil explora-tion and production operations and most of its holdings in related businesses. With the purchase of East Resources, Shell will acquire 650,000 net acres of Marcellus shale rights in Pennsylvania, West Virginia and New York, and 1.05 million acres in total" ("Shell Will Buy East" 2010, 1-A). Local boys done good indeed.

Other stories I had been hearing began to make sense. I remembered the informational meeting held by the Marcellus Shale Committee in the Wellsboro High School gymnasium, where many of the audience's questions focused on why East was not making its lease payments. When I looked up the newspa-per report, I recalled that East was offering lessees a chance to collect higher royalties in exchange for lower lease payments. In other words, East was trying to hold onto its cash. According to the *Wellsboro Gazette*, part of this was due to "the recession and drop in natural gas prices" (Kennedy 2009, 1-A).[4] From 2008 until 2009, gas prices dropped from $13 per thousand cubic feet of natural gas (Mcf) to $4 per Mcf.

No matter what the reason, the fact that one of the major gas companies in the area was scrambling to cover its financial obligations did not reassure me. I wasn't bothered that East was at risk financially—that was its problem—but I was concerned about the long-range economic impacts. What would happen to all the people employed by East? How might such economic sketchiness affect the way people saw this place? Were we on our way to becoming one of the small, decaying towns I saw on old Highway 15 after the bypass was built? Would Lilace and I invest in property that would lose its value? We were assuming it wouldn't, but now I wondered. These stories clashed with the Marcellus Shale Coalition's and politicians' stories about a brighter, safer, cleaner future. The *Gazette*'s reporting made the industry sound shaky, and I didn't want to buy a house in the country as the industry crashed down around me. That's like reaching for your water bottle when you are plunging down a steep, rocky section of trail on your mountain bike. There's a good chance you're gonna fall.

—◦—

The *Gazette*'s reporting confirmed the stories I had heard about East's finances, but my satisfaction was short lived. Now Shell was moving in. While I hoped Shell execs might be more conscientious than the smaller companies like East, I suspected they would care even less about Tioga County itself. At least East was a Pennsylvania company. Shell is headquartered in the Netherlands. Though some might see Shell's presence as lending stability to the region, I saw its arrival as a bad sign.

I knew of Shell in part via its poor track record when it came to human rights in Nigeria where it drilled for oil and gas. Some people went so far as to accuse Shell of being complicit in the hanging of Ken Saro-Wiwa, a writer and community activist in Nigeria who led protests against Shell's oil operations for the way the company treated the people and the land (Doyle 2009). As the story goes, Shell was not happy with the activist who threatened to upend its economic relationship with Nigeria, and Shell paid the Nigerian government to provide protection for the company via its military and police. After proving successful in his campaign against oil extraction, Saro-Wiwa was arrested, given a farce of a trial, and hanged. Human rights activists and Saro-Wiwa's family claimed that Shell could have interceded on Saro-Wiwa's behalf, but it waited until after Saro-Wiwa was convicted, which proved too late.

I agreed with the people who accused Shell of being complicit in murder and who pointed out that Shell could have exerted pressure to stop the execution of the activist. You didn't have to be a genius to see that Shell stood to gain by Saro-Wiwa's execution, because it meant one less questioning voice in the region. Of course, in the United States, we're a little more subtle with our corporate terrorism. So I greeted Shell's arrival with mixed feelings, hoping it was as conscientious as many people claimed yet, given what happened in Nigeria, concerned about its ethics. I knew Shell had a longer reach than East, and I assumed its pockets were deep enough to make happen pretty much anything it wanted.[5]

One of my biggest concerns about Shell stemmed from the fact that it was even further removed from this place than East. What Shell people knew about the place is what they had learned from maps, seismic testing results, contracts, lease agreements, and the like: in a word, symbols. These symbols, though, gave an impression of the place that differed from the locals' lived experiences. I suspect Shell employees toured the area extensively, trying to get a sense of the place, but the main office is 3,700 miles away, separated from Tioga County by the Atlantic Ocean. Sure, Shell opened an office here called Shell Appalachia—I can see it from the front porch of our house—and, sure, it hired locals familiar with the area to do much of the work. But that doesn't mean they know the place, except for the resources they extract, nor does it mean they care about it.

Not long after we moved to the country, Shell stamped its authority on Tioga County in a big way by paving three miles of Charleston Road, a road about a third of a mile as the crow flies from the Whitney house. It's important to know the back story. Context matters for rhetorical acts.

One major complaint about the industry from the outset was the truck traffic. The number of trucks passing through Mansfield's stoplight from 2009 to 2011 could be as many as one hundred trucks an hour.[6] Early on, many of these trucks passed through Wellsboro where Route 6 turns north at the Wellsboro Diner. Always sketchy in terms of traffic, the intersection marked the north end of Wellsboro's Main Street. As county seat, Wellsboro projects a more refined image than Mansfield, and, like in Mansfield, the traffic bothered people. Residents began pestering the county commissioners for a truck bypass to lessen the amount of traffic rumbling through. Since much of the truck traffic was heading north of town to load frack sand at the train station, the logical solution was to send trucks around Wellsboro via the Charleston Road/Catlin Hollow Road cut-off. Once this route was decided on, Shell paid to have this section of Charleston Road upgraded and paved.

Shell coughed up some serious cash to pave the road and posted signs to let the community know about it. Usually we think of rhetoric as having to do with words and images—symbolic acts— yet here was an act that involved a company completing the physical act of resurfacing a road. So how is paving rhetorical? Let me count the ways.

First, Shell's action provided a service to the community that, without a doubt, benefited Wellsboro, and it also benefited Shell. Shell kept the peace with the community. As the county seat, Wellsboro serves as the location for the Tioga County Courthouse, the local hospital, several assisted-living homes, Gmeiner Art and Cultural Center, Hamilton-Gibson Production Community Performing Arts, a host of restaurants, lawyers' offices, local and state politicians' offices, and the gateway to Pennsylvania's Grand Canyon, all arrayed within walking distance of downtown on sidewalks lit by gas lamps at night. Yes, gas lights. The town hosts several popular events every year, like the Dickens of a Christmas Celebration, the Laurel Festival, the Susquehannock Trail Performance Rally, the Endless Mountains Music Festival, and other cultural and athletic events. Those events confer on Wellsboro the status of the cultural center of Tioga County and make it a destination for tourists and locals alike. Such events, however, lose a bit of their magic when triaxle water and dump trucks and eighteen-wheel sand trucks and flatbeds rumble nearly nonstop through town, exhaust spewing, spitter-valves spitting, brakes squealing, springs squeaking. Shell stood to benefit from alleviating some of the truck traffic, and it showed that it was willing to work with the community soon after it moved here by respecting the community's concern for safety and appearances. Put another way, the company recognized that, by paving the bypass, it could boost its image in the community's eyes. Shell paving Charleston was an act similar to East giving $50,000 to support Tioga County's 4-H Club, and many gas companies undertook similar actions. The paving job made the road safer for trucks and cars, and it made the Wellsboro intersection less crazy. To be sure, there were real benefits.

Shell paying for new asphalt on Charleston Road sent another message: we've got deep pockets, and we know it. This was the dimension of the message that bothered me most. Roads are public property, yet here was a private company paying to resurface one. Gas companies are held responsible for the road damage they cause, and many roads they have destroyed have been rebuilt better than before. But Shell made Charleston's resurfacing happen in part because it wanted to assuage complaints in Wellsboro. I found its willingness to throw around big bucks to improve relations with the community unsettling. I had always suspected that oil and gas majors had deep pockets—that they are among the most profitable businesses of all time confirms this, as does the amount of money they throw at problems to try to cover them up[7]—yet I had never seen anything like this kind of money in action. I appreciated the new pavement once it was complete (as a driver, not a cyclist—more on that in a moment), though I wondered about Shell's motives. I wondered how local politicians and other government officials might respond to requests from Shell after the road was resurfaced, since they knew Shell had dropped several hundred thousand dollars on asphalt and quieted some voices in the community. I suspected that Shell's act would make it harder to criticize them. No one likes driving on a rough road, and here was the new kid on the block, a really big kid, smoothing one out.

Before we moved to the country, I knew about the Charleston/Catlin Hollow cut-off. The roads linked Route 6 and Highway 287. Cyclists around here prefer Charleston/Catlin Hollow because the roads get us off Route 6 onto a relatively traffic-free route to the roads in northwest Tioga County. When I moved to Pennsylvania and started riding Charleston Road regularly, I saw it as a typical country road, a narrow two-lane with rough pavement and little in the way of a shoulder passing fields and houses. The pavement was so rough in places that I steered toward the middle of the road to avoid crashing. Taking the lane didn't matter because there were so few cars.

Employees from HRI paved Charleston Road for Shell over the course of a few weeks. With the asphalt in place and the lines painted, they packed up and left. All that remained was a lovely new road surface, at least as far as this cyclist was concerned, and plywood signs announcing who did it. The trucks started growling up Charleston to the four-way stop sign in Whitneyville, and soon the plywood signs disappeared. Not long after, my cycling buds and I stopped riding Charleston Road, except maybe on Sunday mornings when traffic was lightest, because of the trucks.

As I've said before, I trust truck drivers, but the number of trucks lumbering past me and my cycling compadres caused me to suck my shoulders up around my neck in fear. Given its narrowness and its steep grade near Hills Creek Road, too much can go wrong on this section of Charleston Road. When we climbed the steep hill on the newly paved section, trucks passed us excruciatingly slowly, which meant the trucks spent long moments in the oncoming traffic lane. Sometimes, trucks would almost stop in the road, because traffic coming down the steep hill prevented them from passing us with any momentum. That meant the truck drivers spent an even longer time trying to pass us on a hill with reduced visibility and a speed limit of 50 mph, which meant cars and trucks descending the hill would be flying, which also meant if a truck was beside a cyclist, the driver climbing the hill had three choices: (a) slam on brakes and stop on the hill, (b) hit the oncoming vehicle head-on, or (c) swerve into the cyclist. None of those are good options. Every time I climbed Charleston, those scenarios ran through my head, and I felt like I was riding on borrowed time. An important road to us became unrideable, which meant the northeast part of the county was off limits as well. While I don't blame Wellsboro for rerouting the trucks, Shell's largesse didn't benefit cyclists.

Catlin Hollow Road was resurfaced not long after, and the

trucks multiplied. I'd sit on my porch, look out across the bottomland and cemetery toward Charleston Road, and count ten, fifteen, twenty trucks over the course of thirty minutes. I heard them at three or four in the morning, when I got up to use the bathroom or respond to students' papers.

—o—

At a national level, the gas industry portrayed our neck of the woods as The Next Big Thing and eventually reached the university, though not in a way I expected.

As I recounted in chapter 1, the rumor mill suggested the university was in dire financial straits. In 2010, the rumors hit the news. On May 26, 2010, the *Mansfield Gazette* reported a projected $4 million budget deficit for the university, which led the administration to consider curriculum changes and laying off faculty and staff (Kennedy 2010b, 1-A). The fact that my job suddenly felt less secure became a part of my argument for not buying a house in the country. While rumors swirled about university finances, I watched the industry spend hundreds of thousands of dollars on extracting gas in Tioga County, a jarring clash of economies. I didn't want to lose my job, nor did I want my colleagues, some of whom were close friends, to lose theirs. *If only we had some of that gas cash*, I'd think, followed by, *screw that. They'll want something back*. I wasn't sure I wanted to keep my job if the university sold out to the industry.

Turns out the gas industry wanted something from the university anyway, money or no. They wanted faculty to keep their mouths shut.

I wasn't the only academic interested in the natural gas industry. In June 2010, *The Chronicle of Higher Education*—*The New York Times* of higher education—published a report by Scott Carlson called "Colleges Atop Gas-Rich Shale Weigh Offers From Drillers." Carlson's report focused on four colleges sitting above the Marcellus shale, one of which was Mansfield University. Carlson began the report by focusing on Keystone College's Kevin Wilson imagining a "different future" for his school (2010, A1). "A game changer," Wilson called it, an echo of the industry's rhetoric of the future. Later in the report, Carlson talked with then MU provost Peter Keller, who appeared in the photo at the top of the story conversing with a gas worker. Keller told Carlson that Mansfield was a public university, and even if it could lease its gas rights, it did not guarantee that it would benefit. That this boom was occurring while Mansfield discussed laying off faculty and cutting staff was not lost on Keller. Carlson quoted Keller, "The irony associated with this is that while we sit in the midst of this energy boom, [. . .] we face the biggest financial challenges that we as a university have had in 30 years" (A13).

The disturbing aspect of Carlson's interview occurred a paragraph later when Keller suggested that faculty at Mansfield who had questioned the gas industry had hurt possibilities for the university to benefit from relationships with it. Carlson explained how Mansfield, which was attempting to brand itself a public liberal arts university, lacked vocational or professional degrees that directly benefit the gas industry. Keller pointed out that the university sought ways to meet the industry's needs through such programs as watershed management, but there was still work to be done.[8] Keller also pointed out that the university had reached out to the industry, only to be met with a chilly reception. Carlson reported,

[S]ome academic responses have angered the industry, the provost says. Professors on the campus have held lectures and shown films about the impact of gas drilling on the environment and on local communities. Subsequently, when the university approached gas-drilling companies to discuss partnerships that might help the community, the business officials were frosty.

"Sometimes there is a message sent saying that if we're not on board with what is happening, they are not interested in cooperating," Mr. Keller says. "It's both subtle and not subtle, but it's pretty easy to read between the lines." (Carlson 2010, A1–A13)

When I read about the industry's reaction, I thought, *assholes*.

I value my work at the university in part because the university values researched arguments. We think about stuff, weigh evidence, and create knowledge and understanding. I appreciate that my colleagues and I can follow our research agendas where they take us. Sometimes we hit dead ends. Sometimes we add something meaningful to our understanding of what it means to be human. This matters at a time when knowledge is increasingly beholden to special interests, like the gas industry, and Keller's comments suggested that universities are not impervious to outside influences either.

You won't be surprised to learn I was one of the professors who questioned the industry—emphasis on "question." I never called for an outright ban on fracking, though I was critical of the way the industry stood to make profits that would not stay in the community and how the industry would affect the place, and I questioned its story about being The Next Big Thing. That's what rhetoricians (and other academics) do. Most of the time when I spoke publically, my audiences were ten or fifteen people, if that, at small, regional English conferences. Sometimes I wrote letters to the editor or to local politicians. I was no Bill McKibben, though when MU's president called me to get my perspective on gas drilling, I told her there was no way the industry knew what the long-range effects of drilling would be. The science wasn't there yet. When natural gas drilling came up in my classes, and it always did, I mediated rather than weighed in with my thoughts, and I made sure all perspectives were aired. Many of my students were directly affected by the industry, ranging from parents working for the industry to grandparents leasing land to people working for the industry themselves. I found it more interesting to hear their stories and read their papers than to raise my questions. These were people whose lives were being affected on a daily basis by the drilling and the rhetoric of the industry. Many saw the industry as a mixed blessing, hopeful and distrustful at the same time.

Another incident that I suspect contributed to the industry's frosty reception of MU's administrative outreach occurred when the chair of the geography department, Dr. Russ Dodson, showed the documentary *Split Estate*, a movie set in Colorado and critical of the natural gas industry. I was in the audience the night Russ showed the documentary, and he stated several times before pushing "play" that was he not advocating for any view of the industry. He added, "I don't have an opinion on the gas industry." Instead, he said, he was offering one perspective of the gas industry—a perspective, it turned out, that raised important questions about the nature of gas rights and the effects of pollution on people living near well pads and compressor stations. *Split Estate* was highly critical of the industry, though it lacked the emotional punch and flaming faucets of Josh Fox's documentary *Gasland*.

I found myself conflicted and a bit peeved about the industry's response to my university. On the one hand, the fact that the industry was concerned about some of the faculty's responses suggested that maybe the industry wasn't telling us everything, confirming my suspicion that drilling wasn't as harmless as it claimed it was. On the other hand, the industry was spending lots of money, and MU sure could have used some of it. I care about the university and my work with the students, and I care about telling the truth as I see it, a hard thing to do when my job might disappear. I also care about my kids' health and the health of Tioga County. I recognized that losing an income can place different burdens on a family, not all of them healthy. I understood that the industry's cool reception to faculty critiques was coercive rhetoric, similar to but not as subtle as Shell paving Charleston, and meant to bend the university to its will.

Carlson ended his report by discussing how Cornell University, about an hour and twenty minutes northeast of Mansfield, was handling the gas boom. The contrast with Mansfield and the other colleges mentioned was stark. Unlike Mansfield, a university on its way to laying off faculty and staff, Cornell had the luxury of creating a committee to study the natural gas issue and who recommended that Cornell allow drilling only if it contributed to their "sustainability and climate neutrality efforts." Not surprisingly for Ithaca, New York, the liberal stronghold where Cornell sits, the public protested against drilling prior to hearing the recommendations. Carlson quoted Susan J. Riha, co-chair of the committee: "There are people in Ithaca who are resistant to the idea of another industry in the area," and she added that Ithaca was "10 square miles surrounded by reality." Riha pointed out that upstate New York contained much poverty and many people desperate for work, conditions similar to those found in rural Pennsylvania. Carlson gave Riha the last word: "From the point of view of something that could bring in large revenues, this is the biggest thing in a long time. . . . A lot of this just comes down to who is going to be getting the benefits, who is going to be paying the costs, and who is going to accept the risks." *Easy for you to say*, I thought. *Your university doesn't need to beg the industry for money.*

To her credit, Riha recognized that, while the natural gas boom offered something positive to communities, there would be downsides. But her words sent the message that people of Ithaca were not thinking carefully about their opposition to growth in jobs and the economy—that old "future-holds-promise" frame—whereas I'd argue exactly the opposite. The people of Ithaca were being realists, while the industry was presenting these ideal views of the future it promised, which had found traction with some smart people. I wanted Riha to come on down to the Whitney house for a few days to experience some reality. We could sit on the porch, drink beer, and count gas trucks. Then we could drive around and look at drill rigs, pipeline construction, and road destruction. Maybe I could introduce her to some friends who were pissed about the way the industry treated them and their land. One friend got so mad at the repeated hassles with the industry he told an industry rep that "if you come back, you better bring the highway patrol with you."

Though Carlson doesn't mention it, Cornell was not immune to industry pressure either, but it had the financial wherewithal to not need the industry's money. Some Cornell professors raised questions about the industry that did not line up with the story being told by the Marcellus Shale Coalition and other industry mouthpieces. When Francis and I attended that meeting in 2009 in Waverly, New York, sponsored by the Cornell Cooperative Exchange, we heard rural sociologist Jeffrey Jacquet give a perspective on the industry that challenged what the industry had been telling the public, especially in terms of leases and social effects. But the rhetorical acts that created the loudest complaints from the industry came from two Cornell professors: Robert Howarth, the David R. Atkinson Professor of Ecology and Environmental Biology, and Anthony Ingraffea, who holds the Dwight C. Baum Professorship of Engineering.

As the gas industry boomed in Pennsylvania, Howarth and Ingraffea became known for questioning whether the process was as clean as the industry claimed (Howarth, Santoro, and Ingraffea 2013). Ingraffea lectured often in New York, and videos of him debating pro-gas opponents appeared on YouTube. Ingraffea had an engaging personality and a background in oil and gas geology and engineering. His credentials satisfied the academic in me, lent him credibility, and gave weight to his questions about the story the gas industry was telling. He was the first person I heard who responded publically to the gas industry notion that fracking had never polluted an aquifer or water well by pointing out the industry drilled through the aquifer *before* it put in the casing, creating all sorts of possibilities for pollution to occur.

Howarth and colleagues' research tried to account for the amount of methane, the main constituent of natural gas, that escaped during the drilling and transportation processes, what business ecologists would call a systems analysis (Goleman 2009). As Howarth pointed out, the issue was that methane is a much worse greenhouse gas than carbon dioxide, because it captures 100 times the heat of CO_2. Given the state of the global climate, that is not good.

—◇—

Howarth et al.'s research hit the public in 2011. The gas industry did not respond frostily but hysterically. The Marcellus Shale Coalition and another lobbying group called Energy In Depth hammered the research. In a post on the former's website called "Five Things to Know about the Cornell Shale Study (Courtesy of Energy in Depth)" (2011), the lobbyists provided readers with a preemptive rebuttal of the problems with Howarth et al.'s research. Though the post raised some good questions, it was peppered with phrases crafted to discredit the researchers. The word "studies" appeared in quotes, which suggested they weren't real, and it included a lengthy section on Howarth's natural gas activism.[9] Scientific research appeared from other institutions, like Carnegie Mellon (see Jiang et al. 2011), that questioned their results.

Over time I realized that two of the forces wrestling for control of the public conversation about Marcellus shale development were Penn State and Cornell, two top-tier research institutions about 200 miles apart. More a redneck hippie than a redneck farmer, I trusted Cornell's research more than Penn State's, though I found myself buffeted by the different messages, the mental analogue to strong winds pushing me around on the bike. I knew what my priorities were—I wanted to preserve the health of my place and my family—but the conflicting academic reports made the ground I sent roots into seem friable. The experience changed the way I viewed universities, and I started questioning the worth of the institution, defined broadly, I'd dedicated my professional life to. I wanted clarity. I got mud.

One of the first rumblings I heard from parties interested in something other than rampant drilling came in the form of an informational meeting with environmental lawyers in the high school gymnasium in Galeton, Pennsylvania, in January 2011. Full-page ads in the *Wellsboro Gazette* announced "ATTENTION PENNSYLVANIA RESIDENTS: Does Natural Gas Drilling in Your Backyard Concern You?" This statement was followed by text describing a meeting to be held by Weitz and Luxenberg, P.C., a law firm that promised to present a different perspective on the industry. The ad announced the firm had earned Erin Brockovich's endorsement and included a small photo of a woman who barely resembled Julia Roberts, followed by the quote, "I know and work with this law firm and I trust them."[10]

That Weitz and Luxenberg scheduled the meeting suggested at the time that the public was beginning to question the industry's actions. It was no accident that the firm used a picture of a woman who fought in a modern-day David and Goliath story about a big corporation mistreating the land people lived on and the air they breathed at the same time that landowners and lessees in Tioga County were beginning to see their own or their neighbors' rights trampled or land polluted. Or both. The reality of natural gas development differed from the image created by the industry and politicians, a problem we symbol-using and -misusing animals have to watch for constantly. Weitz and Luxenberg saw an opportunity in shifting public perceptions and injected its voice into the cacophony dominated largely by the industry. The firm crafted its message in such a way that the audience could identify with what the lawyer might have to say. Anyone affected by or worried about the industry could identify with Erin Brockovich.

By this time gas drilling had become a part of everyday life in Pennsylvania, and it promised to intensify, especially if the proposed 360,000 wells were drilled across 93,000 acres. These numbers spun through my head as I walked through light snowfall to the car on a bitterly-cold Thursday night. We'd been living in the Whitney house for less than three months, and I wanted to hear the environmental law firm endorsed by Erin tell people how they could protect themselves from gas industry malfeasance. Or how they could sue. I drove 30 miles to Galeton through thickening snow, relieved to know that locals were seeking out info from someone other than the industry, though the advertisement carried a whiff of ambulance chasing. The Black Keys droning in the background, I wondered what I would learn and whether I'd make it back home that night. Given the subject of the meeting, I couldn't help but wonder for the umpteenth time what we had done moving to the country.

In Galeton I hung a left off Route 6 onto Bridge Street and saw that the Galeton Area School parking lot was packed. People parked alongside the road and walked through the snow to the gym. I was early, and the lack of parking suggested that locals were interested in hearing what these lawyers had to say. I hurried through the cold to the gym, a larger version of the one in Waverly, and found a seat near the back. The place was crowded with people dressed like the people at the Wellsboro meeting— Carhartts (I wore mine), hats, high school hoodies. As people chatted around me, I looked toward the front, trying to figure out who was who. I saw a young, black-haired man wearing skinny jeans and a tight black sweater with his shirt tails tastefully protruding from beneath the hem. He wore the pointy sideburns of an urban hipster, provoking one old guy sitting near me to ask his friend, "Reckon he's the lawyer?" Turns out, the blonde woman wearing the black power suit was the lawyer. She looked slightly harried, like an elementary teacher facing a rowdy class, but when she started to speak, she took control of the room. Class came to order.

Julie LeMense, an environmental attorney for Weitz and Luxenberg, explained that her firm had been working with a few locals on lawsuits stemming from the industry polluting air and water. Though she couldn't mention the nature of the lawsuits, she said that her firm and the plaintiffs thought other people may be interested in hearing in general terms what sorts of legal actions could be taken against the industry by landowners whose property had been affected by gas drilling. She ran through a catalog of issues, including disregarding the agreements in the lease to polluting the landowner's property. As she talked, she referred occasionally to a green binder that contained more information about what her firm could do for landowners. She noted at one point that she did not have enough binders for everyone in the room, but if people gave their name and contact info to her paralegal, Urban Hipster, her firm would mail binders to them.

During Q&A, people asked about a range of issues, including whether her firm could force the industry to start paying them for their leases. I noticed right away that, unlike the Wellsboro meeting, there was more anger in this crowd, more concern about social and environmental costs, more stories about poor treatment. The lawyer handled these questions gracefully, referring to her original presentation about helping people who were having trouble with the industry regarding primarily environmental concerns. After answering a number of questions, the lawyer volunteered to answer more questions individually. A crowd swarmed the front, looking to snag a binder. Others clustered in small groups, talking about hunting and wondering aloud why they should trust a lawyer. I thought about requesting a binder but decided to beat it back to the house. I walked out into a full-on snowstorm, flakes swirling around me like the conflicting messages I heard about the gas industry. This time, at least, I heard a message that came from a party that questioned the industry instead of cheerleading for it. That was refreshing, given that most of the rhetoric I had encountered in Tioga County did otherwise. I left the meeting cautiously optimistic that the majority of locals in the Galeton auditorium/gymnasium recognized that they had been told one thing about gas extraction but the reality of the work was something else. As I drove home, I replayed the discontent I saw in Galeton and questioned our decision to buy the Whitney house as the car fish-tailed up snow-covered Charleston Road. But I also looked forward to eating dinner on the front porch after the snow melted and "chillin'" took on a different meaning.

—◦—

While all this rhetoric was flung about the county from 2009 to 2011—the industry attempting to convince people to see the place as a resource, the naysayers questioning the industry's perspective—I kept riding my bike. The crunching gravel under my tires; the wind whistling through my helmet; the fatigue building in my legs; the chance sighting of a grouse, bobcat, or bear; the bullshitting and sprinting with my friends kept my worries burned off. I found it easier to face what was occurring around me if I wore myself down physically on a regular basis. Plus, I was able to see what was happening on the ground, checking the paper-thin line of my own particular life against the rhetoric telling me how I should see it. The rides also reminded me that we lived in a beautiful, though not spectacular, place.

Cycling as a retreat began to change. On many rides, the sight of a well pad or the throaty grinding of a drill bit cutting into the Pennsylvania earth snapped me out of the present and into guessing about the future. My rides were no longer about the next hill, a stunning sunset, or a deer sighting, but about things I couldn't predict or control. I rode my bike to recharge, yet the industry's presence made it more difficult to get that same boost. I chose rides that avoided sections of Tioga County because I wanted to avoid the trucks and the dust. Some days, when I felt more combative, I pedaled roads I knew to be crowded with trucks, my way of saying, "Hey, gas dudes, I live here." Mostly, though, I sought quiet rides, intent on pedaling out the stress of a demanding and possibly shaky job in the midst of an extractive industry drilling full bore into a future about as clear as flowback water.

My rides included a weekly Wednesday night ride called Man Night, where I de-stressed by racing my friends around the roads of Tioga County. Man Night was born in 2007, prior to the gas boom, when bike shop owner Tom Oswald and I talked one evening about how much we disliked driving 12 miles to Wellsboro for Thursday evening group rides with the Twisted Spokes group. Tom and I believe that one reason to ride a bike is to stay out of a car as much as possible. We also believe that we should have as much fun on bikes as possible. Racing friends is mega-fun. We solved our driving problem by starting our own "race night." We shared our plans with two close cycling buds and began to meet on Wednesday evenings at the bike shop at 6 p.m. Soon we had a regular crew of four to ten riders, though the core group consisted of Tom, Francis, Dan, and me: the Four Horses' Asses of the Apocalypse. Wednesday nights soon claimed a reputation for being painful.

Most nights our rides left me physically wasted, until I wrapped my hands around a post-ride beer and replayed the ride's heroics with the other Asses. The best rides, meaning the most painful, occurred in July and August when it was the four of us and maybe Josh and Jared and Eric; it stayed light until after 9:00 p.m., and we were fit from riding all summer. We'd push each other nonstop for between 40 and 50 miles, never letting up until we sprinted for the Mansfield Borough sign on our way back to the bike shop. I often ended these rides on the verge of puking.

When it got dark and cold in the fall, we hung the road bikes on the wall and rode our cyclocross bikes, lights strapped to the handlebars, on the dirt roads crisscrossing the county. When the cold and snow drove us inside, we rode our wind trainers in the bike shop.[11] As always, we ended with beer at Changos Cantina or Yorkholo Brewing, about six doors down from the bike shop. Our conversations revolved around the night's ride and a number of other topics: who would win the Giro d'Italia or the Tour de France, problems with colleagues or students, books we were reading, movies we had seen, politics, races we trained for, fitness or lack thereof, and beer we had tried. Sometimes we covered all of these in one night. The conversations were (and still are) always energetic and irreverent, the verbal equivalent of our rides. We give each other hell every chance we get. On riding: "Yeah, Francis, you sprint like a glacier." On being long-winded at parties: "I opened a beer, sat back, and Jimmy just started talking." On aging: "Dan's an eighty-year-old trapped in a sixty-year-old body." Man Night connects me to my place and my friends, a much-needed weekly ritual. I plan my week around the ride and the conversation to follow. As the gas industry ramped up production, that became part of our conversation too.

One Man Night in July 2010, seven of us pedaled away from all the messages about retrenchment, economic impacts of gas extraction, Shell buying East Resources, and negative environmental impacts to thrash each other over 40 miles of hard riding around the Arnot Loop. We had had a blast—lots of hard climbing, sprinting for borough and township signs, and some fast pacelining.[12] My heart rate and breathing had rarely slowed, and I could feel the deep quadricep fatigue that accompanied riding at my limit. Less than three miles from the bike shop and beer, we declared a truce and cruised in a loose group down the slight incline of Canoe Camp Road through fields and past farmhouses, chatting and joking, a flock of Lycra-clad turkeys picking their way through a field. We laughed about close sprints and sneaky attacks, and praised Francis and Tom for putting the hurt on us on the Arnot Road climb. One of the slowest climbers in the county, I had hung with the group well, which meant I was getting fit. I was stoked and had forgotten all about the gas industry. Then I saw a white conventional Mack pulling a 45-foot tank trailer speed around the curve in the middle of the road straight toward us, headed for the one-lane bridge we pedaled toward.

Riding toward the back of our group, which was spread across half the road. I yelled, "TRUCK!," grabbed my brakes, and steered toward the side of the road. More shouts of "TRUCK!" followed as three of my buddies crossing the one-lane bridge grabbed their brakes and steered toward the right side of the bridge and a shrinking margin of safety. Seeing us, the driver slammed on the brakes and shuddered to a stop a few feet before his side of the bridge. Dust raised by his locked-up trailer tires floated north across the road, glowing in the sunlight. No one was hit, but it was close.

My friends and I rode past the idling truck on a narrow ribbon of pavement, through the dust cloud, and out toward the open road. I ignored the driver and tried to process what had just happened. Though I was too far back to be hit, my friends toward the front were not. They avoided injury because they were on bicycles and able to respond quickly. And they were lucky. *Goddamn*, I thought, *that was close*.

Our banter about the ride's argy-bargy[13] turned to disbelief. "Jesus!" someone finally said, "That was close! Did someone get a license plate?"

I turned to Eric, the truck driver in the group, "What the hell was that guy thinking?"

Eric said, "He was going too fast and should have swung wide before the curve." We all turned inward again, tires hissing on pavement, beer and heroics forgotten. A meek toot of the truck's horn chased us down the road, an apology of sorts from a guy who knew he had screwed up. We pedaled the two miles to the bike shop slowly, the boisterous conversation muted by the close call. We didn't mention our Man Night heroics again until the beer flowed.

There were other close calls during this time. Once, a red pickup passed five of us pacelining though Blossburg, only to turn right, across our path, as we sped through town at 25 mph. Since we were inches apart, we yelled, grabbed brakes, and steered for any available piece of asphalt. No one fell.

I have ridden my bike thousands of miles in North Carolina, Nevada, and Pennsylvania, and I've never experienced closer calls than I have in 2009 and 2010. Before that, Pennsylvania had been the best of the states I had ridden in in terms of traffic. In many ways, it still is. Before the industry came to town, I would ride for two or three hours and see fewer than five cars. Sometimes there was so little traffic I wondered if we had been invaded or something. To the industry's credit, 99 percent of the trucks who passed us were conscientious and respectful, giving us a wide berth. I appreciated their care and always waved. But those close calls changed the tenor of our rides and my perception of the place.

Prior to the near-miss with the Mack, Canoe Camp Road held a different meaning for me. I had ridden that road a number of times (and still do), encountering traffic, chatting with friends, racing, and watching deer and turkeys running through the fields or hawks surfing the air currents. After that Man Night in July, however, Canoe Camp was marked with an unpleasant memory of what could have been. This was not the future in Tioga County I had in mind.

Memories are funny things. They give me a sense of belonging, a sense of a life lived in a place. The quality and quantity of my memories in a place correlate with how much I feel rooted into the place. The places I feel most at home—the western North Carolina mountains, Reno, Tioga County—are the places where I've created and lived the most memories, especially outdoors. Those are places where I can pedal a familiar road, hike a familiar trail, or walk a familiar yard and catalog all the specific places where something happened. *I crashed my bike there. Got caught in a storm there climbing with Lilace. John and I drank a ton of beer there one night. Nearly hit a ruffed grouse with my bike there. Saw a pileated woodpecker fly over my head there. Dan crashed there. Papa had his stroke and fell there.* I've been to places more spectacular than western North Carolina or Tioga County, like California's Yosemite Valley and Colorado's Rocky Mountains, and I have great memories of those places, but I experienced them as an outsider. I remember the spectacular moments, like climbing the

Southeast Buttress of Tuolumne's Cathedral Peak in California or mountain biking the Monarch Crest Trail in Colorado, the latter a huge contrast to the almost humdrum experience of riding, say, the Mansfield bike path. I'm not in the spectacular settings of California or Colorado long enough to lay down the everyday memories that give me a sense of deep belonging.

Back in Greek and Roman times, rhetoricians relied on their memory to give their speeches. No teleprompters. Some of these speeches lasted hours, so speakers had to figure out a way to memorize all that material. They came up with the method of loci, or the practice of tying sections of the speech to specific rooms in a house and then mentally walking through the house in a particular order and "picking up" each section of speech. While I'm not trying to memorize a speech, my memories of Tioga County work in a similar way by providing a structure of my belonging to this place by preserving my history here, a history created by memories attached to specific places. Every time I drive, hike, or pedal through a familiar landscape, I run through a version of my story there as I move past the places where I've created memories. Of course, as I mentioned earlier in the book, I recognize that my memories are shaped somewhat by what I brought to Tioga County, like when I focus on forests and wildlife instead of houses. Since I've moved here, I've created more memories, and the quantity and quality of those memories attached to this specific place comfort me and reassure me that I am home.

One thing I've learned about living with the gas industry and thinking about how the industry has affected my sense of place relates to the role bad memories play. I don't think only good memories are necessary to experience a positive sense of belonging to a place. I still remember the day a friend and I were riding when he told me that our cyclist bud Tom Kaufmann had hit a car that turned in front of him and died. Tom left behind a wife, two kids, and a big hole in the cycling community. Occasionally, I pedal past the place where Tom hit the car, and I always think about the times he and I raced each other and how something we both loved could so quickly turn tragic. But Tom's death didn't affect my sense of belonging to the place. Even though I was deeply saddened by his death, Tioga County still put off a good vibe for me. What this tells me is that good memories and bad come together to create my sense of this place, and that lived history gets inscribed onto the landscape the same way words get written on a page.

Most of my memories of Tioga County are good ones. Backyard cookouts. Watching my kids play baseball or swim. Riding my bike or hiking with my wife. Pedaling into Mansfield in the dark after a 200-mile ride (in cyclist speak, a double century). Receiving tenure and promotion. Seeing bears and bobcats. But the gas industry moving into Tioga County was like someone adding a room, and maybe an entire wing, to my memory house, one with out-of-plumb walls and uneven floors. The industry's presence discombobulated the story I was writing for myself and my family from the memories I'd laid down in this place. As the industry trucks lined up, the drill rigs sprouted, and the rhetoric flew, my roots pushed into different ground.

5   Red, White, and Bluewashing

✳   One Saturday in 2010, I was driving east on Route 6 out to Bungy, a green dot on the map eight or so miles east of Mansfield consisting of a bridge, a church, and a couple of houses. Gabe and I were headed out to see our friends, the Yorks. Thad and I would drink beer and debate the various methods of smoking pork or merits of various beers while Abe, Thad and Nikki's son, and Gabe ran wild over the Yorks' property, fighting off an imaginary invasion from an imaginary enemy. The kids had a good place to make a stand: the custom home Thad built sits down a hill from the gravel road. On the downhill side of the house, the porch runs the length of the house and catches the afternoon sun. At the south end of the house, there's a small alcove and patio, where we sit. Spanned by a bridge Thad built, the "crick" gurgles by about 50 feet away. Kingfishers patrol the creek, chattering machine-gun support for the boys' battle. The chicken coop and Nikki's garden sit across the bridge in a grassy field. Behind them, a tree-covered mountain rises several hundred feet. I've spent many hours at this house, drinking beer, smoking pork and venison, and telling stories, a place I now call the Bungy Vortex because I get sucked in and can hardly ever make myself leave. The place's peacefulness chased by Thad's good beer and venison backstrap cooked rare pull me down into my chair like the willow's roots across the way sink toward the creek. I always stay longer than I plan.

After Gabe and I passed through Mansfield en route, we saw a drill rig on the north side of Route 6, "See that rig, Gabe?" I asked, pointing.

"Yeah," he said. "It's got an American flag on it."

"Sure does. Why do you think that is?" Though I had seen flags flying from the top of many rigs, Gabe's observation pushed my brain in several directions at once.

"I don't know."

I thought about trying to explain how many of the gas companies in the area were American companies and how they wanted to appear patriotic, but I decided that a seven-year-old on his way to play Army with his buddy wouldn't give a damn about that. Taking the easy path, I told him we'd talk about it sometime and hoped internally their imaginary war wouldn't be over oil. Gabe and Abe have plenty of time to worry about that. But Gabe's observation made me think about all the American flags I had seen crop up in Tioga County since the industry moved in. They flew on drill rigs and outside offices and were stuck to pickups, water trucks, dump trucks, and sand trucks. With a strong military history, this part of Pennsylvania has never been shy about flying Old Glory. Hell, when we weren't flying the Jolly Roger at Halloween, we flew the American flag at the Whitney house on our 20-foot aluminum flagpole, something I never thought I'd own. I found, though, that I like the sound of a flag popping in the breeze, accompanied by the clang, clang, clang of the clips banging against the pole. Our flag marked us as part of something larger.

Gabe's observation in mind, I paid more attention to the American flags I saw blooming around the county alongside the drill rigs. I understood why some companies flew the flags. East Resources was based in Warrendale, Pennsylvania, and Chesapeake Energy was based in Oklahoma City, Oklahoma. As red-blooded American companies, their flags made sense to me, and I appreciated that they were American companies keeping their wealth in the United States.

When Shell opened its office within eyesight of our house in the country in 2010, I noticed it flew an American flag too. That didn't sit well with me, because the flag obfuscated the nature of

Shell's relationship with Tioga County. Shell is based in the Netherlands. There are many foreign companies at work in the Marcellus. Schlumberger, another major player, is based in France. Talisman is based in Canada; Reliance, India; Statoil, Norway. I'm not naïve about how the global economy works, but any foreign company flying the American flag creates a different impression of the company with the public. I suspected many of the people working for Shell Appalachia were Americans. I knew some of them. Seeing the Shell Appalachia sign, however, made me feel like we were a Shell colony. Sure, America benefits from gas drilling in some ways, like jobs and cheaper prices (though I'm not sure the latter is a benefit, given the state of the climate). I also suspected that if Shell needed to ship natural gas to other countries to make a profit, it would. That's how the global economy works. Energy independence be damned.

That Shell flying the American flag was doing its job was driven home one day when I mentioned to a colleague that Shell was based in the Netherlands. "Really?" he said. "I didn't know that." After that, I made it a point to tell people every chance I got that Shell wasn't made in America.

—o—

Like words, images shape our perceptions, functioning the same way as words. The American flag is an image, a symbol that carries a lot of meaning. Agents, like Shell, use images in ways that direct the audience's attention toward particular attitudes or beliefs. Since we've mostly been focusing on words, I now want to focus on images. Both words and images are ubiquitous in rhetoric, complementary forms of symbolic action, and both can carry multiple meanings. That means that industries choose carefully the images they use in order to direct attention toward the meaning or end they desire. The gas industry understands the power of words *and* images, and it uses this understanding to its advantage.

The problem with images is that they often confuse an issue by oversimplifying it. Using specific images can make it hard for the public to get good information, because the images tap into attitudes it already holds. In terms of rhetoric, images bore into our minds and release certain attitudes or beliefs in the same way gas drillers drill into the shale and free the gas. Images frack the jumble of thoughts we carry around and draw forth associations deeply embedded in our gray matter. We encounter this phenomenon all the time.

I don't watch TV much, but I've seen an image from an advertisement for the drug Cialis that I can't seem to shake: a camera shot from behind a man and a woman sitting in separate claw-foot tubs resting outdoors on a deck. Placed in the lower half of the frame, the couple holds hands while the camera records the sun setting over a forested, hilly landscape spread out before them. They gaze into each other's eyes. They're naked. It's getting dark. We know what's coming. As we view this image, the announcer reads the list of side effects, which include that a man shouldn't take Cialis with high blood pressure. Then there's the possibility of a perma-erection requiring medical intervention. This could seriously curtail someone's cycling.

I associated the couple-in-tubs image with my own memories of romantic situations leading to intimacy with my wife. I felt warm, aroused, and wondered what my wife was doing. Not to be too graphic, but we'd be in one tub. But when I tried to remember the side effects of Cialis, I couldn't. I had to Google them. The image of the couple in tubs did what it was supposed to do—it embedded itself into my head and drew forth certain memories that drowned out the scary side effects. When I checked on the side effects, I found that they were worse than I thought. Positive images override scary messages.[1]

—o—

When Gabe saw the American flag, he saw a symbol that held some meaning for him and that shaped his perspective on natural gas drilling. Even at a young age, Gabe associates with the American flag and patriotism, though he understands it on a simple level. Nor is he immune to associating it with the industry in some vague way, which shapes, however slightly, how he views the industry. (Same for us.) For Gabe, the American flag is an unequivocal good. Symbol-using animals make these associations all the time, and the gas industry is quite good at using images to form certain associations. They use images strategically to draw on deeply held cultural and historical beliefs that say, in essence, "Look at me. I'm a great company, and I'm making the world a better place."

Part of the power of the industry's go-to images is the way they bring two deeply held cultural beliefs to the surface of my mind: nature as a resource and nature as something to preserve. The images create a particular perception of people who work for the industry, as well as of Tioga and the surrounding counties, one that is pro-America and pro-gas. The images the industry uses serve as visual terms or shorthand for a set of values that apply to our twenty-first century circumstances while at the same time drawing on key cultural associations from our pasts. The Cialis ad works the same way. The promise of romance occurs with the popping of a pill and draws on memories from earlier times. ("Remember that night at that B&B in Valle Crucis, honey?") Industry's images draw on stories we tell ourselves about our past as a nation, like Manifest Destiny or patriotism, though they work as shorthand by making a complex idea appear much simpler.[2] At the same time, however, images are sloppy, which means there's wiggle room in how we understand them, so we have to think carefully about how they are being used.[3] Perhaps counterintuitively, that sloppiness contributes to their power. Images prod us to understand what they represent by linking us, the audience, through loosely shared but not clearly defined beliefs, beliefs that incline us to think or act in a particular way. And images can present certain beliefs as oppositional, such as patriotism and environmentalism.

I've found the natural gas industry draws on three images repeatedly: the roughneck (a term that describes people who work in oil and gas fields), the pastoral, and the American flag. By looking at each, we can gain some idea of how these images work to forward the industry agenda, confuse the public, and shape our views on how this place should be used.

—◦—

When I used to work construction, one of the things I loved most about the job was getting off work and going to the bar. Whether strawberry margaritas at Anita's in Herndon, Virginia, Falls City beer at Tom and Trudy's in Alderson, West Virginia, or Sam Adams at Greg's in Surfside Beach, South Carolina—it didn't matter. Walking into a bar in dirty, sweat-stained clothes and ordering a beer at the end of a long day hanging sheetrock, shoveling out a ditch for a waterline, or framing a deck marked me as a guy who worked with his hands. A masculine guy. A tough guy. I looked at the golfers and realtors and small-business owners in their knit shirts, hands manicured, and knew I was superior. *You guys are soft. Swinging a 28-ounce Estwing framing hammer all day would kick your delicate asses.* Eventually, I became one of those guys in a knit shirt, so I looked for other ways to keep my connection to those days working construction, like felling trees with Eric or building a chicken coop with Thad.

We have a strong attraction to people who can build things

with their hands that comes to us from the stories we tell ourselves about the first settlers in the New World or the cowboys
who tamed the West during Manifest Destiny. Like settlers, cowboys, soldiers, and truck drivers, people who work construction
are tough, physical people who have something tangible to show
for their efforts at the end of the day.[4] As a college professor, I
would argue I still work with my hands, but it's not the same. I
don't sweat while grading student papers, attending meetings, or
crafting my own writing—except metaphorically. I don't mash my
fingers, race to beat the rain, or feel that deep muscle fatigue that
comes with framing a condo or planting treated 8"×8"×16's for a
deck. That's probably why I ride a bike so much, especially when
it's below freezing. I still want to be seen as "Tough Guy."

The way we perceive construction workers and other people
who work with their hands is based on stories we tell ourselves
about them. These stories have deep roots. I've already mentioned
Manifest Destiny. There's also the Protestant work ethic.[5] On
occasion I see a bumper sticker proclaiming "My Boss is a Jew-
ish carpenter,"[6] though, in my experience working construction,
most people didn't care what Jesus did except for exclamatory purposes (e.g., "Jesus fucking Christ, that beam was heavy!"). Other
hard workers in stories include Joe the blacksmith from Dickens's
Great Expectations, the early Jurgis from *The Jungle*, hardworking
drillers in *Oil!*, the steel mill workers in *The Deer Hunter*, the cowboys in *Lonesome Dove*, Matt Damon and Ben Affleck's characters
in *Good Will Hunting*, Jon Bon Jovi's character on *Ally McBeal*,
Joe the Plumber. I'm sure there are others. Not all of these characters are fine examples of humanity, but they all share a certain
cachet because they knew the meaning of hard, physical work. I
see Daddy in those types of characters. He drove a big machine
hauling all types of materials through all kinds of weather under
all sorts of deadlines. While he didn't necessarily swing a hammer

or repair the plumbing, he hauled food that fed people and concrete reinforcing wire that helped build bridges or shelter people. None of those jobs are easy. We value hard work—or, at least, what we call "hard workers."

The natural gas version of these masculine, hardworking guys is the roughneck. When we encounter images of roughnecks in the media we see big, burly guys wearing hardhats, reflective clothing, and deep tans, like the guys drinking beer in the local bar Changos. Like construction workers, roughnecks are associated with hard, important physical work that serves a need and can be dangerous. In the images it uses, the gas industry taps into the esteem with which we view hard work in order to attract workers and to persuade the public to respect the work. Such images appeal to the masculine American desire to appear tough.[7]

The Marcellus Shale Coalition (MSC) understood how the image of the roughneck played out in the public mind, as well as the guys' minds who worked on the rigs.[8] MSC's website includes an image of a roughneck on the employment page. We see a white man posed on the left side of the screen, body facing to the viewer's right and head turned toward the viewer. Chin jutting, he squints in the sun. He wears a white hardhat pulled low and a black jacket with the collar turned up. His posture and facial expression send a message of seriousness and challenge. The guy, and he is a Guy, seems to be saying, "If you're not serious or can't take it—and I'm not sure you can—don't apply. We're tough." The image is accompanied by the words "RENEWAL" and "PROSPERITY." The former word implies that becoming a roughneck can lead to a new life, a rebirth, the proverbial turning over a new leaf (an interesting choice of words, given that crime rates often spike during a boom), while the latter suggests such a job will make you wealthy.[9]

While there is no doubt in my mind that a roughneck has to be tough—seeing a drilling rig, lights ablaze, at two in the morning in subzero temps convinces me—the image chosen by MSC taps into public beliefs or attitudes about the importance of hard physical labor that go way back in American history to Manifest Destiny. In 1893, when that frontier was settled and we struggled to find something else, historian Frederick Jackson Turner argued that the taming of the frontier created a new kind of American democracy. In his "Frontier Thesis," Turner (1921) argued that the hard work and violence required to settle America created a new kind of American identity. This identity was a masculine one and built on deeply held cultural totems like the frontier, cowboys, and the Wild West. This kind of thinking creates the archetypal rugged individualists we now admire and was the basis of the infamous Marlboro Man. MSC's use of the roughneck image appeals to the strand of rugged individualism that runs through our culture, a strand that supports our beliefs in personal freedom, self-reliance, competition, and little government oversight. The image of the rugged individualist counteracts the "feminization" of males who hold desk jobs in cities. Concern about the feminization of men drove Teddy Roosevelt and educator G. Stanley Hall to discuss at the turn of the twentieth century ways to ensure men became "manly" men: the wilderness cure for overcivilization. MSC's image echoes those concerns.

Of course we don't have to go back to the late 1800s to see the hold such archetypes have on our perceptions. MSC's roughneck reminds me of the famous black-and-white poster of Clint Eastwood's 1976 outlaw character, Josey Wales. Same steely gaze. Same jutting chin. Hat pulled low. Only Wales has a beard and a couple of six-shooters. Our modern rugged individualists ride Harleys, climb big mountains, make it big in business (Aubrey McClendon comes to mind), proudly own guns, drink whiskey, drive big trucks and ATVs, eschew helmets, and wouldn't be caught dead using the word "eschew." We link the traits of rugged individualists with certain kinds of work, rightfully or not, because Manifest Destiny and Turner's Frontier Thesis have been powerful forces in our cultural imagination. Drawing on these forces, images of roughnecks project notions of charting new ground and combining freedom, hard work, and a sense of progress to create something great. These images romanticize the roughneck and attempt to make the less attractive aspects of the work, like freezing your ass off on a drill rig, into a virtue. The images of roughnecks conjure visions of hard workers taming the frontier. But they don't head West,[10] because the new frontier is buried a mile underground.

—o—

Farms are everywhere in Tioga County, a fact that feeds Lilace's and my attraction to this place. I process chickens at the Chesters' Always Somethin' Farm. We visit other farms, like the Websters' Hillstone Farms, the Englands' Glenfiddich Farm, or Andy Lyons' Spring Meadows Farm, to pick up produce or pork shoulders, or just to show the kids a real live farmer in action. The visits make visible the way we depend on this land for much of our food. We connect with the place by consuming food grown here and supporting farmers who practice the kind of farming we preach about. Mike Chester says, "I'm trying to make good soil." Good soil is a good place to grow roots.[11]

When I ride my bike, I ride by dozens of farms spread over the county. Two I see often are across the hill to the north of our house. Set in a rolling valley centered between three ridges, the farms consist of big farmhouses set near even bigger barns, both surrounded by fields dotted with cows. One has fifteen or twenty Massey Ferguson tractors of various vintages parked around the yard. Built higher up near the southernmost edge of the valley, the other farmhouse has an expansive view north of pastures rolling away until the mountains rise and the trees reassert themselves. Every time I pedal past these farms, I see them from a distance as pastoral landscapes, as symbols of rural simplicity and peacefulness. I don't see the mud, the broken-down equipment, the aging barns, and I don't hear any tractors idling or milk pumps thrumming until I pedal between the houses and the barns. Because I'm steeped in pastoral imagery, the farms take on the qualities of a pastoral landscape painting from the Hudson River School or maybe a passage from James Fenimore Cooper's *The Last of the Mohicans*. Paintings and books like these present us with a view of farmers peacefully working their fields while fireplace smoke streams gently from the farmhouse nestled in a beautiful landscape setting. Such images suggest an idyllic existence, which is then reinforced when a writer like Cooper portrays the farmers as simplistic and noble. What these artists and writers leave out is the dirt and the shit and the hard work found on every farm, work I can see and smell as I pedal past.

I romanticized farming because I had read many books, seen many movies and works of art, and heard lectures extolling the virtues of peaceful retreats to the countryside that suggested genteel country living. I grew up around people who saw trips to the country as an escape. But farming is more difficult than many of our cultural artifacts have led us to believe. The perception that we can escape to the country, like Tioga County, is facilitated in part through the notion that farmers live peaceful, easy lives and encounter few problems. The natural gas industry understands this, so it taps into the power of pastoral imagery to shape the way we see drilling.

When we look at pastoral landscapes, like farms, we are looking at an image that, like the roughneck, has deep roots. The idea of the pastoral grew out of literature as far back as Virgil and Shakespeare and often involved shepherds tending their sheep. Since then, the definition of pastoral has changed, though it still suggests a simple rural life, peaceful, punctuated by hard but satisfying physical work. Though this perception is beginning to change with the growing awareness of the struggles of farmers to keep their farms producing and the lack of any of these qualities in large agribusinesses, the notion of farming as an innocent, idyllic enterprise persists, because farms exist in what we might call a middle landscape (Scheese 2002, 7). They aren't wilderness, but they aren't the city either. In the geography of our minds, farms exist somewhere between Philadelphia and the Adirondacks or San Francisco and the Sierra Nevada. This concept of a middle ground fits well with our beliefs about gardens and brings Eden to mind. Pastoral does contain "pastor" after all, and the pastoral evokes longing for a simpler life before the fall.

If I'm being honest with myself, I'll admit that one reason the Whitney house attracted me in the first place was its pastoral qualities. The house and property offered quiet, privacy, some wildlife, trees and fields, and a chance to escape the complex world I live in. The big old brick house set back from the road surrounded on three sides by trees, the paths cut through the five-acre field out back, the old barn ruins on the west side of the driveway, the space for a garden and a chicken coop, the deer, bears, owls, turkeys, coyotes, woodcocks, and red-tail hawks wandering or gliding by—all these suggested a place where I'd be able to leave work and other responsibilities behind. I wouldn't spend as much time in my office.[12] I'd have to attend fewer meetings. I could sit outside and not hear *people*. I'd live in a retreat. Hot damn!

Though neither urban nor wilderness, I thought the Whitney house contained enough of both for me to live a middle existence, providing me with the benefits of a retreat that was a short drive from the beer store. Of course, the reality is anything but. Thanks to Wi-Fi and cell phones, students and colleagues can reach me any time. It takes two to six beers to cut the grass, depending on how long the grass is and how thirsty I am. Chickens need feeding, kids need driving to swim practice and rehearsals, and the trash does not roll itself to the curb. So the Whitney house is not a pure retreat, but when I'm sitting around a fire in the backyard with the Horses' Asses after a forty-mile ride, some Flower Power in the beer fridge, watching and listening to the wind rustle the willows, I settle into a peacefulness I didn't feel in our old house. Part of that peacefulness comes from my sense that I'm doing what I'm supposed to do in a pastoral setting. Feeling at peace. Retreating. But, as many have said before me in more eloquent terms, this is so much bullshit. We can't ever truly escape our complex circumstances, but we sure as hell can find places to recharge. That's what the Whitney house became for me.

—o—

The pastoral can be represented by the farm, located near Uniontown, Pennsylvania, opening this chapter. To the right of the industry's tanks, we see silos, barns, mowed fields, trees, and cumulus clouds spread out across a blue sky. There's a sense that the land is domesticated, but it retains some wildness as well. Even with tanks present, the photo evokes the sense of pastoral paintings and literary descriptions that suggests that landscapes should be used and preserved.

MSC evokes the pastoral as well when it promotes natural gas by using photos showing drill rigs in close proximity to farms. Like the photo of the farm near Uniontown, we see a farmhouse and barn in the distance and well-manicured fields surrounded by forest—a middle landscape. MSC frames one photo so that the rig appears front and center. The rig dominates the image, making it a prime example of what Leo Marx calls "the machine in the garden." MSC's image introduces the technology of natural gas drilling—drill rig, trucks, storage tanks, and so on—into a landscape otherwise seen as simple and peaceful. Such images draw forth our competing but deeply held cultural beliefs that nature is something to be used and preserved. The landscape and well pad in MSC's photo look pristine, even though a tremendous amount of dirty, back-breaking work was required to establish and maintain the fields and the pad and to operate the rig. The rig and pad appear like a still-life, a painting created by early artists who portrayed heroic, simple farmers peacefully working their fields. Shot on a bright, sunny day, MSC's photo provides the impression that the work is clean, just as farms appear to be from a distance before I ride up to them. We can't see any dust or hear any drilling, fracking, or swearing roughnecks. We see a clear, crisp image that suggests the process is clean and so safe that farmers can work their fields up to the edge of the well pad.

I call these types of images "industrial pastoral." Such images evoke the pastoral response of the peaceful rural lifestyle coupled seamlessly with extractive technology. Our view of the landscape is framed such that we see the drill rig as an aesthetic object within a pastoral setting. We're not close enough to see the work, the mud, the mixing of chemicals, the pulsing hoses, the pipe drilling into the earth. No trucks or people move in the frame. The image is static, spiffed up for the guests who visit. We look down on it from the perspective of gods (which, in one sense, we are) admiring our handiwork. Even though the rig has punctured the illusion of the idyllic farm, it appears to fit harmoniously with the field. Such images help us reconcile our competing beliefs of nature-as-resource and nature-as-preserve.

We see similar images of drill rigs in the press, though the press's images indicate that the process is not as benign as MSC's PR photo suggests. For example, one image from *The New York*

Times shows a flyover shot giving us a god-like perspective of a rig, roads running in either direction, wastewater pit in the background. A garage sits in the lower right corner, which suggests a house nearby, and a house or a barn appears in the lower left corner. The rig is centered in the photo, though the low light and busyness of the landscape mean it lacks the orderly aesthetic of MSC's photo. The photo suggests that parts of this landscape are worked, though it's not clear we are looking at a farm. Yet, for all these differences, the *Times* photo records an image of a drill rig and well pad remarkably similar to the MSC's, an issue I address shortly.

Shot in the American West (maybe Wyoming?), a photo from ProPublica projects a vision of natural gas that resonates with the idea of taming the frontier. We don't see a ranch house or livestock. Instead, we see a long shot of a drill rig positioned artfully in the frame in morning or evening light with a sage mountain range glazed pink in the background. It's easy to imagine a Josey Wales-esque roughneck out taming this new underground frontier. The rig is distant enough that we can't see any type of work occurring, so there's no sense of the full impact of the industrial process. Looked at one way, the news photos suggests the same aesthetic as MSC's.[13]

PR photos are different from news photos, though I find the similarities between the photos worth thinking about. While we can't separate them completely from their contexts, the photos accompanying *The New York Times* and ProPublica articles suggest that the rigs mar the landscape, yet the photos also present the rigs as aesthetic objects. Such images suggest that technology and landscape can come together in benign ways. Even though the texts accompanying the news photos are reportorial, not PR, the reports' images work in a way to help us reconcile the contrary impulses of preserving nature and using it. After all, if we remember images better than texts, these images can be seen as similar to Cialis's bathtubs. All three photos amplify MSC's message about nature-as-resource by tapping into our cultural beliefs. I don't think *The New York Times* or ProPublica intends for its images to be advertisements for the industry, but the images project a certain view of the industry that simplifies the complex relationships between nature-as-itself and how we use it. Leo Marx would call these images the "technological sublime" (1964, 194–5). If the sublime suggests awe in the face of dark, crashing seas or craggy, fearsome, looming mountains, the technological sublime represents the power of technology to imprint itself on the viewer and the landscape, overwhelming us and suggesting that we are both powerful and powerless.

I confess I feel a twinge of awe every time I see a well pad with a drill rig carved into the side of a mountain, like the one way up on the side of a tree-covered mountain outside Waterville, Pennsylvania, or the rig lights south of us shining brightly enough at night to create what locals call the "Marcellus Borealis." I react similarly when I see a conventional Peterbuilt or Kenworth with the huge square grill, polished chrome bumpers, and oversized fuel tanks blast past me on I-81 when I'm driving to North Carolina. Our technology is impressive for what it enables us to build. And to destroy.

By creating the "industrial pastoral," the images of the drill rigs on farms help us reconcile the contrary impulses of loving nature and using it. Couple this with the idea of the work that roughnecks do on the rigs—good, old-fashioned, masculine work reminding us of Manifest Destiny—and we begin to see how such images present a particular view of natural gas drilling that ties into contradictory beliefs about how we use nature.

—○—

As I explained in chapter 4, Shell bought East Resources a few months before we moved into the Whitney house. Soon after, it established an office about a mile away from our new house. One of Shell's first acts involved erecting a sign saying "Shell Appalachia, Tioga Office" and raising an American flag. Now we know Shell's home office is in the Netherlands, but the Tioga County office gave the impression that this was an American company. Remember my colleague who didn't know Shell's home country? This is not to say that Shell doesn't spend money here or employ people who live here. But between the name, Shell Appalachia, and the flag, Shell projects the image of a highly patriotic company with America's interests at heart, a powerful message in a rural part of Pennsylvania where many people have served, are serving, or will serve in the military. The flag aligns Shell with patriots, an act I question, though I think it's a smart move by Shell.

I find "patriotism" to be an incredibly complex word. It can mean almost anything to anyone, and it can refer to a group or an individual. After 9/11, American flags proliferated in the weeks following, and we came together as a country. The word "patriot" was on almost everyone's lips—understandably so—and anyone who questioned the prevailing view of taking the war to the terrorists was not a patriot. In a different context, however, like on the issue of gun control, it can be seen as patriotic to question any laws restricting access to firearms, an impulse that grows out of our notions of rugged individualism. These collective and individualist frames show how patriotism can be used to support collective action ("One Nation under God") or individual actions ("Keep your hands off my gun!"). Regarding natural gas, some people see it as their patriotic duty to lease their land, while some see it as their patriotic duty not to. I'm bothered by the idea that patriotism is linked to any kind of extractive industry. Patriots give

Photo by Jimmy Guignard

rather than take. And while the industry may give us jobs, lease money, and a clean-burning fuel (the extraction of which is not so clean), I'm not sure that, on balance, those outweigh the social and environmental costs.

No matter which side of the gas leasing divide people fall on, one thing is certain: it's hard to criticize "patriots." Shell is not the only company to recognize this. Whether foreign or domestic, many of the natural gas companies I have seen have American flags flying outside their offices or stuck to their trucks. The flag aligns the companies with American beliefs, an act that glosses the complex social, economic, and environmental issues surrounding the development of the natural gas industry. The companies may be sincere in their patriotic beliefs, though I have a hard time buying that regarding Shell, and the American flag shields the companies from tough questions. We don't question patriots, especially in times of crisis. While the gas industry boomed here, the rest of the country wallowed in an economic crisis, the perfect time for the industry to use an image of patriotism to move itself forward.

One way the American flag shields companies from tough questions is by symbolizing a nation, not a region or county. Yes, we might each think that where we live is the perfect embodiment of what the American flag represents, but that impulse does not negate the idea that the flag was created to stand for all states collectively, and all the land in those fifty states, whether rural northcentral Pennsylvania, New York City, or any other place within our national borders. In that context, Shell's use of the flag contributes to the notion that Tioga County is abstract, a blank space on the map. The American flag represents our collective national identity, which is constructed on a diverse geography populated by a diverse people. It doesn't stand for any one place but all of them, so it functions in part by glossing differences. I don't fly the Guignard flag in my yard, or the Whitneyville flag, or the Tioga County flag. I fly the American flag. It identifies me as a part of something larger, much in the same way that Shell's American flag pledges some sort of allegiance to America.

One problem I have with the natural-gas-as-patriotic frame has to do with the fact that patriots often make huge sacrifices. Using the flag as a marketing tool belittles the sacrifices—sometimes of their lives—made by patriots. Since I've moved to Tioga County, I've gotten to know many veterans, and I now understand the nature of their sacrifices—something I've always respected in the abstract—in a much more visceral way. A flag on the top of a drill rig twists the nature of those sacrifices into an unrecognizable form for me.

Plus, Tioga County is not at war, though at the height of the industry's rush in 2010, it felt like we were being invaded, with trucks streaming over our roads like Patton's tanks across Italy. We're not a population oppressed but a group of people living our lives in the peacetime safety of the northcentral Pennsylvania hills. Though I suspect some people felt liberated by the gas boom, especially when the paychecks started coming in, I didn't. There was nothing to save us from, except perhaps the industry itself, but the idea of patriotism and the presence of American flags conjure up images of sacrifice and make it easier for the nation to think of this place as a "sacrifice zone." Using American flags that tapped into patriotic zeal creates a perception of Tioga County as an abstract zone where the industry works in order to preserve an "American" way of life. It's more difficult for a community to push back against patriotism than against big multinational corporations drilling holes in the ground for resources and profits.

—○—

We've seen how the industry uses the images of the roughneck, the pastoral, and the American flag to persuade the public to perceive the industry's work in a certain light. We can also see where the industry brings this Holy Trinity together to great effect in one advertisement. My favorite version comes in the form of a billboard advertising Chesapeake Energy, found just south of Mansfield on Old Highway 15. On the left side, the words "THE ANSWER TO FOREIGN OIL" blare from the billboard in bold, light-blue text on a white background, followed by a smaller font just beneath proclaiming "American Natural Gas." Chesapeake's logo completes the text, all centered within the two-thirds of the billboard covered by white. On the right one-third of the billboard we see a short portion of a white derrick silhouetted against a blue sky with an American flag flying prominently in the foreground. A light-blue band spans the bottom of the billboard, tying the text and the images together. The colors used on the billboard project boldness, purity, and cleanliness, and the image on the right side draws on the images of the roughneck, the pastoral, and the American flag to align Chesapeake with those cultural beliefs.

Photo by Jimmy Guignard

The rig suggests the roughneck because, without him, it wouldn't be there. The blue sky hints at the pastoral impulse—it never rains on a pastoral farm—while echoing the blue flame of burning natural gas. The whites and the blues suggest purity, another hallmark of the pastoral until you get close enough to the farm to smell the shit. The American flag flying in front of the rig suggests, obviously, patriotism. Combined, the three images pose a kind of riddle, to which we get the answer on the left: "THE ANSWER TO FOREIGN OIL." The two light-blue bands extending across the bottom of the billboard look like a fence made of natural gas to keep the foreign hordes at bay. I find the billboard impressive for the way it brings together the Holy Trinity of images and directs the attention away from social and environmental concerns about gas drilling and toward a patriotic, isolationist view of America.

There's an irony here. The billboard brings to mind the industry's promise of jobs. I have ridden by this billboard regularly since it appeared in 2010 or 2011, and I watched Chesapeake take over the yard below it during that time. On any given day, Chesapeake parked over a dozen of their yellow tank trailers, a fleet of white semis for pulling the trailers, and a gaggle of white pickups. During the height of the boom, the lot stayed full, and I figured I'd always be haunted by the specter of Aubrey McClendon and his company residing in my town. But then, out pedaling the Arnot loop one day, I noticed all the gas drilling equipment was gone. Not a trailer or a truck remained. Chesapeake disappeared like a tenant sneaking out on the last month's rent. I took a photo of the billboard on Easter morning in 2012. It had been presiding over an empty lot for over a year, becoming a visual formula for the frustration people felt about the mixed messages sent by the industry.

—◦—

Television shows use images that skew the public's perceptions of events as well. Less than a month after we moved to the Whitney house, CBS's *60 Minutes* gave a report about natural gas extraction in the Marcellus shale called "$haleionaires." Hosted by Lesley Stahl, the report interviewed Chesapeake Energy's Aubrey McClendon about the future of gas, told the story of two newly minted "shaleionaires" who lived above the shale, and questioned the Sierra Club's Michael Brune about negative environmental impacts. I don't watch much TV, but I wasn't about to miss this report. After all, millions of people watch *60 Minutes*, and I knew whatever was said on the show would have a big impact on the nation's view of natural gas extraction. While Lilace put the kids to bed, I cracked a beer and settled on the couch.

The *60 Minutes* report opened with McClendon giving Lesley Stahl a rundown on the scope of the natural gas resources in the

Marcellus shale and then moved into the story of two men who had become rich leasing their property. *Good for you*, I thought. *You got lucky*. The men seemed surprised and attributed their new riches to luck and the Lord. What bothered me about the story, though, was how misleading the story of riches was. By the time *60 Minutes* aired this story, the gas industry had been drilling full tilt in Pennsylvania for about two years. It was true that some people made hundreds of thousands of dollars leasing their property. A student from one of my composition classes who worked as a bank teller told me that he deposited $10,000 to $30,000 checks every month for some locals. "Royalty payments," he said. Friends told me about how so-and-so who lives on Hills Creek Road deposits $50,000 into his account every month for the gas flowing from under his property. Who knows if these stories are accurate, but I did not doubt a few were making plenty of money from leasing. On bike rides, I saw new tractors parked beside old ones and houses being resided or reroofed. Brand new Dodge and Chevrolet muscle cars rumbled through town alongside geezers in brand-new, full-size pickup trucks, trucks I knew would never be used for much more than hauling a bag of potting soil or the occasional deer. The signs were all over: Money was in town.

For every story I heard about Nouveau Riche Guy getting $3,000 an acre to lease his 300 acres, however, I heard two stories about people who had leased their property for $10 or $25 or $50 an acre before the industry metastasized across the county. I knew many people who didn't want to lease at all but felt they had no choice, because the neighbors surrounding them had leased. Stahl's interview with the two old guys who struck it rich resonated and fed the hyperbole and vision of the future that benefited gas industry promoters like McClendon. Given that frame, no matter what *60 Minutes* reported, the promise of riches would taint it.

I've got to give McClendon credit. During his interview with Stahl, he was charming, composed, and enthusiastic, and I understood why people found him believable. In spite of that, McClendon pissed me off when he told Stahl that "In the last few years we have discovered the equivalent of two Saudi Arabias of oil in the form of natural gas in the United States. Not one, but two" ("$haleionaires" 2010). I appreciated the guy's brashness even as I cursed the TV, *What the fuck are you talking about!?* I didn't want my place to be thought of as a "Saudi Arabia"—that's an abstraction for most people in the United States, including me. A source of oil and little more.[14] I wanted Tioga County and the Whitney house to be thought of as a place where I could drill deeper roots with my wife and kids, not as the extractive industry wasteland I imagined it would become. "Fuck that guy," I muttered into my beer. "Asshole." *This is my home.*

To provide "balance," *60 Minutes* brought on the Sierra Club's Michael Brune. Stahl asked Brune about the possible negative impacts natural gas extraction may have on the environment. Brune earnestly rattled off the problems with air and water pollution, and I recognized right away that his presence was more like the fretful adult who urges kids to take their medicine, not the flamboyant, fun-loving presence of McClendon. Though I sided with Brune's concerns, I knew that the cautious approach toward developing the resource would not compare to the excitement of fun and riches offered up by McClendon and the newly rich dudes. Of course, in response to Brune, McClendon stated that there had never been a documented case where fracking caused water pollution. He added, "It's perfectly safe," while the camera cut to Stahl nodding her head.[15]

I don't remember what followed *60 Minutes*' story on the Marcellus shale. I think I stared at the wall, frustrated and dismayed by such a simplistic story about such a complex process. In the

Wellsboro Gazette and other local sources, I could get some semblance of complexity. I wanted to know that the nation was seeing the gas boom as something more complex than a way to make a couple of "blessed" guys rich for doing nothing more than owning land in a Saudi Arabia of the Occident.

The show also provided a great example of Marx's technological sublime. The report shared a series of close-up, medium, and long shots of drilling equipment drilling away, even when the industry was being criticized. The segment's script was split almost evenly between the pro-drilling crowd and those who question drilling, but most of the visuals of drilling equipment mimicked the type of footage we see for muscle cars or models in that we get long shots and close-ups, which present the machines in a flattering light. Call it industrial porn. The footage of the drill rigs becomes the equivalent of the tubs in the Cialis ads. We remember the images of the well-maintained rigs running smoothly and producing gas more than we remember what people actually say. (It's worth noting viewers saw about a minute's worth of outright negative images.)

By the report's end, Lesley Stahl and her producers had given me an image of the industry that appeared positive, one that had me yelling at the TV. The show looked too much like an ad written by MSC, because the positive images outweighed the negative ones, and the images themselves managed to override most of the message. The report did not accurately reflect what I saw happening where I lived.

When we look at the images of the roughneck, the pastoral, and the American flag together, we see three images that complement each other and that tap into deeply held cultural beliefs about America. We value hard work, independence, natural beauty, and our collective identity as a nation, even though we may define each of these things differently. That's why the gas industry uses them so effectively. These images mean a lot of things to a lot of people, allowing enough wiggle room in each image's meaning to tap into the differing attitudes of a diverse people. Though my son may not have thought "patriotism" when he saw the flag, many people seeing the flag will. Each of these images will not resonate equally among people, but all three resonate with larger cultural beliefs that make up our national identity. I would argue that the viewer often doesn't think carefully about the images themselves. I didn't, until my son mentioned the flag on the drill rig, and I began thinking about images as rhetoric. Instead, we get a vague sense that Chesapeake must be doing something right because the Holy Trinity of images align the industry's work with cultural beliefs that have deep roots in the stories we tell ourselves about ourselves.

These images illustrate how rhetoric shapes our perceptions in powerful, subtle ways and why we need to think carefully about the symbolic acts we see. None of the images used by the industry are wrong or invalid or incorrect. There's some truth to them. But the images are used intentionally to bend our attitudes toward particular ways of thinking about drilling for gas. Because the images are so deeply infused into our culture, the work ethic represented by the roughneck, the peacefulness represented by the pastoral, and the patriotism represented by the American flag serve as a type of ultimate term or god-term (Burke 1950, 183–97). Essentially, ultimate terms or god-terms are vague words that carry a lot of meaning for people. Though the American flag seems the most "godly" of the three images, all of the images attach deeper symbolic meanings to what is otherwise a commodity. Put another way, the images create drama around the extraction of natural gas. I can imagine the roughneck in the MSC ad saying, "You're a tough guy. Now, help me tame the frontier for your country." Otherwise, drilling is simply a physical act, like repairing a bicycle or digging a ditch. Granted, the scale or the impacts are not the same. The industry recognizes this and confuses the public discourse by using such images in ways that support the industry's work. The industry's use of images attempts to make drilling for gas seem inevitable. As symbol-using animals, it falls to us to enlarge the context in which such rhetoric is used in order to understand what other possibilities exist. That is, it is up to us to understand the big picture, not just the partial picture presented to us by the industry.

This state of affairs is what makes rhetoric so powerful and so frustrating—our world is shaped by words as much as we shape our world by using them. I'm used to seeing energy industries fly the American flag, so the implications didn't register with me. My son's observation helped me understand that my own attitudes about the environment and nature had blinded me to the patriotic message projected by the gas industry. Patriotism can be a good thing. But understanding rhetoric requires that we actively seek out intended and unintended messages, think about how those messages shape our perceptions, and then decide how we should act. Once you take it on, this is fun, and sobering, work. I'd even argue it's patriotic. Since our understanding of the world depends so much on symbols, we might as well get used to it.

My wife came up with the term "red, white, and bluewashing" to label the way the industry uses the Holy Trinity of images. (Thanks, honey!) Red, white, and bluewashing shuts down discussion or possibilities. It focuses our attention on what our reactions might be as loyal, smart Americans, rather than speaking to us as complex individuals who bring different attitudes and values to gas drilling. Like "greenwashing," red, white, and bluewashing takes the complex and makes it appear simple. Because of this act of simplification, the rhetorician in me sees red, white, and bluewashing as unethical. It uses images in ways that obfuscate complex relationships between land, people, and industry, using patriotic, pastoral, and economic beliefs to divert our attention from what might otherwise concern us. The dude in me who lives here calls red, white, and bluewashing bullshit, because it leads to confusion and uncertainty by injecting misleading information into the bedrock of the communities. It fractures communities like shale, and I'm convinced it's intentional, a PR frack drilled from well-funded well pads built on a web of words, spun by the lobbying groups like MSC and Energy In Depth. I have never lived in a place where I experienced as much day-to-day confusion about so many things, admittedly not all of it coming from the gas industry.[16]

My sense of security depends in part on accurate information, on knowing things, and I believe that the more I know, the more likely I am to live a safe, fulfilling life. Knowing more helps me see more possibilities, more options, which helps me make better decisions for myself and others. I admit that knowing can get maddening, because it means that I have to face the bad along with the good, that I have to drill through misinformation to find accurate information, that I sometimes have to settle for less than what I want, that I always have to be open to learning something new, that I have to be comfortable with change. Sometimes I just want to make a decision, but the world I (and the rest of us) live in is too complex for that. I've found that most of my best decisions come from learning and knowing a lot. It's why I studied for years to be a teacher, why I learned to process chickens I planned to eat, and why I read everything I could about the gas industry before I bought the Whitney house. Not everyone has the time or ability to do this kind of in-depth research, and the gas industry knows that. It counts on it. That's another reason its rhetoric is so effective.

Nothing would suit the gas industry more than to have a bunch of Americans waving the flag in a sacrifice zone. The flag is a unifying symbol, one that provides cover for the industry and makes its work easier. But there's another advantage for the industry in using images like the flag. It aligns itself with an ideal while recognizing that the flag itself is baggy enough to allow for multiple understandings. I think I'm being patriotic when I question the industry, since we have a long history of questioning things in the United States, thanks to our First Amendment rights. When the industry aligns the cultural beliefs in hard work, land-as-resource, and patriotism with the promise of jobs, domestic energy, and economic growth, it creates the perception that it's somehow less patriotic to work to preserve land or to question the industry frame. This results in neighbors arguing with neighbors, community against community—"You're not being a patriot!" "No, you aren't!"—which means we spend our time bickering with each other instead of fully understanding the issues or the stakes involved in drilling. Such contention fractures communities, which works in the industry's favor. MSC and Energy In Depth create the stories they want to tell and to hell with evidence that might disrupt those stories. Their use of images is in line with MSC's mission statement, which claims MSC looks only at the positive aspects of gas drilling. In this case, however, the cheerleaders create an illusion of red, white, and blue goodness via images that taint knowledge like thermogenic methane contaminates water wells.

And who's really the patriot here? MSC's board members and associate members are made up of American companies and companies from the Netherlands (Shell), Norway (Staoil), Canada (Talisman), Japan (Mitsui Oil Exploration), and France (UGI Corporation and Schlumberger). The story keeps changing too. In the four years I have lived in the midst of gas extraction, I have experienced differing messages attached to the same ultimate terms. In 2009 and 2010, I heard "energy independence" on every gas industry believer's lips. Now I hear industry cheerleaders arguing for the benefits of exporting natural gas, because it's worth so little here and so much elsewhere. It's enough to make my head spin, but, then again, a connection to place is about consistency, which the gas industry is not. Unfortunately, the images the industry associates with the gas market are slippery enough to accommodate all sorts of perspectives. We have to constantly pay attention to how words and images are used over time. The industry certainly does.

6 Comfortably Numb

⁜ While the rhetoric and the trucks rattled across Tioga County, I kept pedaling. In 2009, 3,142 miles. In 2010, with the industry booming around me, I rode 3,772 miles. A good year. In 2011, 3,330 miles. By 2012, the industry had slowed down, and I did, too: 2,991 miles. In 2013, another slow year for me, 2,992 miles. Two thousand thirteen was slow for the industry overall, too, though from the front porch we still saw water and sand trucks out on Charleston Road.

From 2010 to 2012, I encountered pickups and water trucks passing me nonstop until I pedaled out onto back roads. Sometimes I didn't escape them then. I experienced two more near-crashes, reminiscent of the encounter with the tanker truck on Canoe Camp Road. In one, Francis and I were riding Highway 14 south toward Troy. As we pedaled past the Troy Fairgrounds at 25 mph, a red Chevrolet pickup passed us. Seeing the brake lights blink once, I slowed to give Francis some room *just in case* when, without signaling, the truck arced right into the fairgrounds' entrance for a natural gas expo, cutting Francis off. The next few seconds are seared into my mind: Francis's bike shuddering through the turn, matching the truck's parabola, Francis fighting to keep control and not slam into the rear quarter panel or slide underneath the rear tires. I soft-pedalled past the entrance to the fairgrounds and watched the truck disappear into a parking lot full of pickups. I saw Francis turn around slowly and pedal back out to Highway 14. *Fucking assholes*, I thought, the spell of 20 miles of pure fun fractured.

Francis was livid when he pedaled up beside me, though not so angry that he was willing to ride down into the middle of a bunch of roughnecks to confront the driver. I didn't blame him. Lycra-clad cyclists riding skinny-tired bikes don't exactly cut compelling figures, as the truck's driver had amply demonstrated.

A hundred yards later, we turned right and pedaled slowly across the pedestrian bridge that cut the corner between Highway 14 and Route 6. Pedaling past the Dandy Mart, we headed east onto Route 6 for a few hundred yards, staying as far right as debris along the shoulder allowed, until we could turn right onto Porter Road, a two-lane nearly devoid of traffic. Eventually, we talked about something other than those goddamn trucks.

Francis and I were riding in late 2010 when he dodged the red truck. The Canoe Camp incident occurred in July 2010. In less than two years, Tioga County went from containing roads worthy of bike magazine photo shoots to becoming a county overrun with traffic. The county still wasn't as trafficky as other places I had ridden, like Reno or Charlotte, but the three years of riding in almost no traffic had spoiled me. Granted, 98 or 99 percent of the gas industry's truck drivers did all they could to give cyclists a wide berth, in part because one accident meant a driver was fired. I believe that most drivers saw us as human beings out doing our thing and treated us as such, even when we slowed them down. Given the number of trucks on the road, I'm surprised that we didn't have more close calls.

But the ones we did have left an impression, though, thankfully, only on our minds. During the gas boom, trucks became a standard part of the rides. I realized how deeply this was the case while out riding with Francis another fall day in 2010. We were heading south on Business 15 a half mile or so past my favorite billboard from Chesapeake when a white pickup buzzed our elbows. The truck was too close—I could have touched the side view mirror—something all cyclists encounter from time to time, gas industry or no. I felt the little shiver that always follows those asinine too-close passes. The driver had room to slide into the center turn lane but hadn't used the extra space. I heard Francis blurt, "I hate those fucking white trucks!" His words pushed me to realize that I had largely stopped seeing the trucks carrying out the industry's work. I had to have a close call. And not just the pickups, all the trucks, and not because there were fewer of them, but because there were so many. Doubtless, the fact that I'm comfortable around trucks and trust truck drivers played some part in the way the trucks receded into the background. That I was acclimating to the industry's presence the way I acclimate on the bike to winter's cold bothered me. Riding in truck traffic early during the boom was like bundling up for November and December rides when temps in the high twenties seem frigid. A year or so into the boom, riding in the truck traffic was like riding in February and March when the same temps or colder don't seem as cold any more. Over time, the trucks became a part of the landscape, and I needed near-misses to see them again.

—◦—

Francis's "fucking white trucks" outburst was still rattling in my head when I met with my Advanced Writing class one week in late October. Taught every fall, Advanced Writing for English Majors is one of the core courses for our major, and it provides a space in which students focus on refining their research and writing skills. Given my academic predispositions, I have designed a class that looks closely at the world from a rhetorical perspective, and we practice this work repeatedly over the course of the class. I introduce students to the rhetorical perspective and assign a lengthy rhetorical analysis. Since much of my research involves rhetorical analysis, I use my own thinking and writing as a model for how academics research, think, and write. Though I find it difficult to open up to students in that way, especially when they see problems with my thinking or a careless grammatical error, I find that they are willing to engage with their own work more honestly and deeply when they realize I don't always think clearly or write perfectly either. I use my behaviors as a writer to model the kinds of inquiry and thinking they need to bring to their own writing. In keeping with my modeling ethos, I sometimes ask my students questions about my research that I don't know the answer to. Being buzzed on Highway 15 and realizing that I didn't see trucks anymore prompted one such question: Is there a rhetoric of trucks?

Eighteen students looked at me. Silence. Then one student asked, "What do you mean, a rhetoric of trucks?"

"Good question," I replied, squinting like a roughneck and looking at the student intently, my standard stalling technique. "I'm not really sure. But I wonder if the gas industry sends some sort of rhetorical message with the overwhelming number of trucks we see around us. Does the presence of all those trucks tell us something besides natural gas is here?"

Not surprisingly, students keyed on the company logos on the trucks, and they complained about the amount of traffic. One student suggested that maybe the number of trucks carried a rhetorical message, because there were so many. "That says something," the student added. "I'm just not sure what." We kicked the question around a while, but like many questions I ask, we ended up not drawing any hard conclusions.

A week later, I received an email from one of my quiet students whom I'll call Sarah. She'd been thinking about the rhetoric of trucks and had an answer for me. She began by stating that the "truck traffic certainly had a rhetorical dimension" but not because the trucks use the roads. She pointed out that the trucks have a practical purpose—they enable the workers to work—and she mentioned that most of the trucks carried logos, which advertised for the industry, saying, in effect, "we've given this guy a job, and he's spending his money here. As are we." Then she wrote

> To me the trucks are also symbolic of the way that the industry treats everything as a resource to be used as needed rather than as someone's home. There has been no apology for the traffic, and while there are known ways to help alleviate the heavy presence of the larger trucks (running more of the large trucks at night instead of during the day or having temporary water piped from a network of ponds, rather than trucking the water in to sites, for example), it seems that the faster, cheaper, etc., way of doing things is generally preferred, which again tells me that the industry is not necessarily respectful of this area and that the trucks are a part of that. About two years ago, before things really took off, my in-laws went to a town hall meeting for a question-and-answer session with an industry representative. He told them that the very first thing that people would notice as the drilling picked up would be the increased traffic accidents and deaths. His reason for this was that people in rural areas do not know how to handle driving with the large trucks and increased traffic. It's our fault, not theirs. There was no responsibility put on the industry. To me that is the most significant and negative rhetorical dimension of the heavy truck presence. When I know that the industry is well aware of the fact that their attitudes and practices regarding their trucks are killing people (both their employees and other drivers) and is unwilling to do something to change it, then they are making a clear statement that says they care less about the value of human lives than they do about time and money.

Much smarter than anything I'd managed to come up with, Sarah's thoughts on the rhetoric of trucks suggested a utilitarian motive that complemented her insight that the number of trucks suggests the industry sees this place as little more than something to be used. Sarah's story about the town hall meeting reflected her perspective as well. I had never heard or read that the industry claimed locals were to blame for the accidents resulting from the increased traffic, and I defended truck drivers for doing what they had to do when Lilace cursed them for partially taking up her lane. I expected local drivers to have to adjust. But the story told by Sarah's in-laws lent weight to Sarah's analysis. It's been my experience that most drivers around here, locals and gas employees (often one and the same), are great, given the narrow, twisting roads and the often sketchy winter conditions.

As I read Sarah's response, I thought about people who saw the presence of the trucks as a positive thing, as progress. Certainly plenty did. As Sarah pointed out, the trucks' logos reveal which companies spent money here. For many, that was good.

—◦—

I found the number of trucks overwhelming at first, both in a car and on the bike. In the car, I'd get pissed when I sat through the Mansfield light three times, which never happened before 2009. Early on, I'd get nervous when I realized I'd turned my bike onto a road with lots of truck traffic. Over time (a year? two years?) I got used to the trucks, an attitude driven home when Francis cursed the truck that buzzed us. His words made me see the trucks that had largely receded in my consciousness the way the pain in my butt recedes as I get more miles on the bike. Realizing I'd gotten used to the trucks bugged me more than the trucks themselves, because it told me I can get used to something I question or oppose. It's hard enough to keep up the energy to question something. It's even harder when I have to keep up the energy to *see* what I need to question.

Differing interpretations create our understanding and misunderstanding of the natural gas industry, and differing interpretations of the truck traffic are plausible. That's the nature of rhetoric, and it can be frustrating. I first complained about the traffic, then adapted to it, and I could see people benefitting from it, though I didn't see any benefit myself. I found my response odd, because I never stopped reading and writing about the industry during that time. Somehow, the words became more real than the trucks themselves.

—◦—

About 6 p.m. on January 29, 2011, Gabe and I loaded the Corolla with chips, kid beer (i.e., root beer), a case of Yuengling, a fifth of Maker's Mark, and warm clothes. We were headed out for a sixtieth birthday party for Eric (aka the Old Man) at his house. Two other Horses' Asses would be there, along with Sheila, wife of one of the Horse's Asses, and whoever else showed up. I told Lilace before we left that we may end up crashing on the couches in the Man Hut, depending on snowfall and my booze intake. Since Gabe was a last-minute addition to the party, I'd recalibrated how much I might drink, but I didn't see the need to call her at 2 a.m. It wasn't like I hadn't crashed in the Man Hut before.

Snow fell thick as I backed out of the garage and steered down the driveway. I decided to take the back way to Eric's, thinking that maybe the dirt roads wouldn't be as bad as the paved ones. Big mistake. Between four and six inches of snow covered Reese Hill Road when I turned onto it. I accelerated at the bottom, silently chanting the mountain bike maxim, *momentum is your friend*, hoping "mo" would carry me up the 10 percent grades. I heard the front tires spinning, heard ice smacking the Toyota's underbody, and felt the car fishtailing as I counter-steered. Gabe chose that moment to ask me a question about the party. "Not now, Buddy," I said. "I've got to focus for a minute." I steered the car as best I could, managing somehow to keep it out of the ditch, hoping no cars were descending. We rounded the curve before the final steep grade and spun our way to flat ground. "That was sketchy, Gabe!" I said. "Could you feel the car sliding?"

"Yeah."

"Crazy, huh? So, what was your question?"

Our next experience driving in snow wouldn't be so lucky.

—◦—

We repeated our spin fest up Eric's driveway, though it didn't feel as desperate. If the car got stuck this time, I didn't care. We could walk to the sugar shack, celebrate, and worry about the car tomorrow. We fishtailed past the sign that states "Hey, asshole, this ain't your fucking land. Go away now or you'll be mistaken for a large, annoying squirrel" and spun over the crest into the parking area between the house and the Man Hut. I backed the car in beside Eric's pickup, turned off the ignition, and climbed out into one of my favorite places in all of Tioga County.

Eric and Joanne's house sits just below the crest of a hill. Dug into the slope on the south side, the log cabin faces forest to the north. A porch runs the length of the house, with steps leading down through flower beds to the driveway about five feet below. The yard contains a small frog pond, a goldfish pond, a vegetable garden, and, in summer, perfectly manicured grass. The Old Man has declared war on dandelions, and it shows. The Man Hut sits across the parking area catty-corner to the house. It's one big room with a small bathroom in one corner and contains a CD player, a television, a gas fireplace, a couch, two captains' chairs from a car, several bicycles, a bike work stand, a weight bench, a beer fridge, chainsaws, and pictures from Eric and Joanne's past. The Man Hut is nicer than some places I've lived. Both house and Man Hut are finished in wood stain, blending into their surroundings. Out back of the Man Hut rests the fire ring, surrounded by picnic benches and stacks of split wood. I have spent hours upon hours around the fire ring, eating, drinking, and bullshitting, and I find this place relaxing as all get out, on par with the Bungy Vortex, the Whitney house, and my grandparents' land in North Carolina. I think it has something to do with nights like the one we were about to have.

Gabe and I grabbed our supplies out of the car and walked past the Man Hut to the old logging road that led a quarter mile down to the sugar shack. The temperature was around eighteen, and snow fell onto the fifteen inches already on the ground. Our boots squeaked as we slipped through the woods toward the flicker of the fire on the trees and Eric pontificating about some past adventure. We rounded the corner of the sugar shack. Eric boomed, "Well, look here! Hey, Gabriel! How you doing?"

"Good," Gabe said. "Happy birthday."

"Thanks, buddy," Eric replied. I walked over, handed him the Maker's Mark, and wished him happy birthday with a hug. I may have whispered "you old fuck" into his ear so Gabe wouldn't hear, though I knew Gabe would hear plenty of salty language before the night was through. We have taught him that context is everything and not to repeat those words.

—◦—

I put down the Yuengling and showed Gabe where he could put his chips and kid beers in the sugar shack, a 10'x10' unfinished room with a big overhang on one side. A couple of old restaurant chairs and scattered newspapers made up the décor. As we headed back outside, I said, "If you get cold, you can come in here, okay?" He nodded, root beer in hand, and led me past the stainless steel vats back to the fire about 20 feet away. Split ash burned brightly in the brick fire pit. On the open side of the fire pit, three logs stood on end, serving as seats. Split firewood was stacked all around us, some on pallets, some stacked in rows taller than my 6'3" frame. Eric, Tom, Sheila, Francis, and Rick, Eric's neighbor, had stomped the snow down around the fire pit. Fire flickered off the trees surrounding us and wind whisked their tops. Gabe took a seat on a log. It was around 8 p.m., and I wondered how long he would last in the snow and cold.

I hadn't seen Rick in a few months. I walked over and stuck out my hand. "How ya doin'?"

"Good, good," he replied, his hand covering mine. Rick's a huge guy with a big beard who carries a cooler of Milwaukee's Best in his Polaris Ranger and a .357 in his back pocket. We chatted a minute before I spied a case of Arrogant Bastard stuck in the snow on the other side of the fire, the Maker's Mark buried beside it. I picked up the Yuengling and carried it to the pile. Setting it down, I opened the case, pulled out a beer, and asked if anyone needed one. Hearing no takers, I opened the beer, shoved it down in the snow on top of some firewood, and grabbed the bourbon. I opened the bottle, said "Here's to the Old Man!" and took a pull.

"The Old Man!" the others exclaimed. I passed the bottle to Eric, who took a swallow and passed it around. The bottle circled the fire, only Gabe and Sheila abstaining. When Francis passed it back to me, I capped the bottle and shoved it back into the snow. Then we settled into some beer drinking and bullshitting about bikes and bike races as the temperature and the snow continued to fall.

As we stood around the fire recounting tales of epic rides and giving each other shit, gas workers drilled the Vandergrift 290 5H well about 1,500 feet away as the crow flies. I knew they were drilling because I had ridden my bike past the well on Ikes Road several times. Plus, Eric kept me updated. This night, the well pad seemed miles away in the dark and cold and the flurry of words around the fire. Almost another world. Eric talked about how he always went to Rochester on his birthday and test-drove a $180,000 RV to, as he called it, "tease the salesman." The conversation drifted away from the RV test-drive like smoke from the fire, then circled back when Eric said, "I love teasing those guys on my birthday. You've gotta try it sometime. I love fucking with them."

I veered from my conversation with Francis to remind Eric that Tom, owner of the local bike shop and frame-builder extraordinaire, was a salesman. I added, "You've got two of his frames in your Man Hut."

Eric looked at me, then at Tom. "Awww, my little buddy," he said. "He sells me all kinds of stuff." He looked at Tom. "You little troll."

Tom laughed. Sheila stood up, put her hands on her hips, and exclaimed, "My husband is not a troll. You take that back." Amusement flickered at the corners of her eyes. Gabe chuckled.

"He is a little troll. Look at him." Tom stands about 5'7" and weighs about 125 pounds.

"He is not," said Sheila. "You apologize right now."

Eric looked at Sheila, then at Tom. Gabe continued to giggle, and I stopped mid-conversation with Francis to watch the rest of the mock drama unfold. Eric staggered over to Tom, arms held wide, and they hugged each other. "I'm sorry, you little troll!" Gabe's belly laugh cut through the trees. Bourbon followed.

—•—

The fire burned low. Eric said, "I hope we can find some wood." The line became one refrain to our circuitous conversation about bike rides, making maple syrup, drinking moonshine, and growing up in Tioga County. Francis piled more wood on the fire.

The ash caught quickly and pushed the cold back a little. Finally, the drill rig made an appearance when Rick turned to Gabriel. "Gabe," he asked, "you want to ride over and see $100 bills shooting out of the ground?" Gabe looked at me. Rick's 4×4 Ranger sat behind us, the fire glinting off the dull green paint and Plexiglas windshield partially covering the cockpit. No doors. Cooler in the bed. Knowing Gabe wanted to ride the Ranger in the snow, not see the gas well, I said, "You want to?" He nodded.

"Let's go then." We set down our beers and walked with Rick to the Ranger. Rick fired it up and drove us through swirling snow along an old logging road to a field where corn grew in summer. We skirted the field, catching a glimpse of the drill rig lights through the trees, before Rick turned down hill, wove through some trees, dropped through a ditch, and crawled across another field in two feet of super-fine snow. Ablaze in lights, the blue and white rig stood about 200 yards away. Rick stopped the Ranger and killed the engine. The roar of powerful engines filtered through the air toward us. "See, Gabe?" Rick asked. "Hundred dollar bills shooting out of the ground."

Jutting around 90 feet into the air, the rig was impressive. Tank trailers, generators, compressors, and trucks clustered around the rig. An American flag whipped and popped from the pole on top. A grinding roar permeated the night, dulled somewhat by the snow falling and blanketing the ground. As I looked at the rig, Dickens's Coketown popped into my head. I watched for Stephen Blackpool walking the pad, but I couldn't see him. Rick no doubt saw money "shooting out of the ground." Who knows what Gabe saw? We sat there another minute looking at the rig, watching the snow swirling between the rig and the Ranger, listening to the bit chew into the earth. I wondered whether the guys working the rig saw us. Rick asked Gabe if he was ready to go back to the fire. "Yeah," Gabe replied, and off we went, spinning back up the hill to a fire pit that struck me as a scaled-down version of a well pad where we engaged in that age-old ritual of gathering around a source of burning energy, conversing and trying to stay warm.

—∘—

Rick's trip started a trend, and the other refrain to our conversation around the fire became "You wanna go see $100 bills shooting out of the ground?" Eric drove Francis down, Rick drove Tom and Sheila down, then Eric drove Gabe and me down again. By this time, he had swallowed a couple of Arrogant Bastards and some Maker's Mark and was feeling no pain. I wasn't either, though I had stopped drinking an hour or so earlier, in part to watch out for Gabe and in part to watch Eric, who was on an epic tear.

Eric, Gabe, and I jumped back in the Ranger about 12:30 a.m. Eric eased out of the fire pit's light, the Ranger's headlights lighting the tracks from previous forays. Because Eric had been operating equipment for over forty years and drove a truck for the Post Office until his company laid him off, I trusted him to not do anything crazy, especially with Gabe in the seat beside him. I was right. He puttered along the tracks, eased across the field into the woods, and dropped down through the drainage ditch into the faint glare of the drill rig, his instincts and experience handling equipment overpowering the booze flowing in his veins. He said, "Look at those $100 bills shooting out of the ground, Gabriel!" Then, as the field flattened, he floored it.

The Ranger bucked and slipped through the snow. Gabe laughed at first, until the snow sprayed between the windshield and the hood, hitting him in the face. In protest, he pulled his knit hat down over his face. I laughed and yelled over the engine, "What's the matter, buddy?" Eric glanced down to see Gabe's cap pulled down and slowed the Ranger to a stop near where Rick, Gabe, and I had stopped before. "Did that bother you, Gabe?"

"Going fast doesn't," Gabe said. "The snow hitting my face does."

"Okay," Eric said. "We'll stop." He pointed at the rig. "Look at those $100 bills shooting out of the ground."

We sat there for a minute, and I wondered how Eric felt about the rig, considering some of those bills ended up in his bank account. My guess from conversations we'd had around fire rings and on bike rides was that he was torn. His father had leased the property before he gave it to his kids, so in some ways Eric had no choice. He has a soft spot for nature, and he worries about climate change. He'd watched the gas workers closely when they worked on his property and fought with them to reroute pipeline around a small wetland. He appreciated the lease money, and I guessed from the references to $100 bills shooting out of the ground, he looked forward to the royalties. But he also knew that he had lost something in return for the windfall, perhaps mostly peace of mind. I sensed a twinge of bitterness often when he talked about the industry, and I sometimes saw outright rage.

This night, Eric seemed giddy at the promise of money from the drilling, maybe the only time I've seen him in that state of mind, and I didn't blame him. He'd served in Vietnam, worked his entire life in construction and the trucking industry, and since losing his driving job to consolidation, had worked seasonally for the Pennsylvania Department of Conservation and Natural Resources. Physically, he's beat up, though he can tolerate more pain than anyone I know. His shoulders were a wreck until surgery, his knees ached constantly, and he often couldn't sleep. His kids lived in San Diego, and he and Joanne strategized on how they could spend time with them during winter, when they had both been laid off from their seasonal jobs. Their plan was to buy an RV, hence "teasing the salesman," and spend each winter in San Diego watching their grandkids grow up.

If anybody deserved a natural gas windfall to ease stress, it was Eric. Yet the promise of gas industry money did not always seem to outweigh the costs. On this night, nobody gave a shit. We just watched $100 bills shoot out of the ground and repeated stories we had all heard before and loved.

—o—

"You ready to go back to the fire, Gabriel?" Eric asked.

"Yeah," Gabe said. Eric fired up the Ranger, put it in gear, and pressed the accelerator. The engine whined, the tires spun, kicking up snow and ice, and the Ranger moved forward about an inch. Eric slammed it in reverse and tried to back out. Same result. He tried to go forward and backward a few more times. We moved maybe two inches. He stopped and put the engine in neutral. "Well, goddamn it, I think we're stuck."

"Let me push," I said. "Gabe, you stay here. Hold on tight." I jumped out, waded through two feet of snow to the rear, told Eric to "hit it," and pushed for all I was worth. Snow and ice bounced off my chest and legs. The Ranger revved, tires spinning. Didn't budge.

"Eric!" I yelled over the revving engine. He let up on the accelerator. "Let me jump in the bed and rock it while you floor it." I climbed in the bed, grabbed the roll bar, braced my feet against the sides, and said, "Go!" Eric floored the Ranger again while I yarded from side to side on the roll bar. The Ranger rocked as snow and ice slapped the sides and underbody. No luck. "Stop, man!" I yelled. "We're stuck good." I started laughing. Gabe sat silently in the front seat, hands wrapped around the bar on the dash. Eric stared down at the steering wheel for a moment, shut off the engine, then hopped out of the cab and started clearing snow from under the Ranger with his arms. I jumped out of the bed to help. Gabe got out and watched. I said, "Whaddya think, buddy?" He shrugged. Once again, we heard the drill rig's implacable grinding and roaring.

After a few minutes of digging, we saw we were hosed in two ways. First, Eric had stopped the Ranger in a swale, which meant the snow was deeper here than in the rest of the field and that the snow sat on ice frozen in the bottom. The Ranger cut its way down into the ice like a drill bit cutting into the earth, settling the underbody on packed snow. We were most definitely stuck. I laughed again when I saw the chained tires sunk four inches or so into the ice. It looked like we had four flats. Eric said, "Reckon we should go get Rick's tractor." I volunteered to walk with Gabe back to the fire pit and tell Rick. Eric said he'd stay with the Ranger. He grabbed a beer from Rick's cooler, opened it, took a swallow, set it down in the cab, and commenced to digging again. When Gabe and I looked back from the top of the field, we could see his crouched figure and snow flying, like a dog digging after a groundhog.

We slogged across the field. I found it tough to walk through the snow, which came up over Gabe's knees. The walk must've been tough for him, too, but he never complained. "How you doing, buddy?"

"Good."

"You ready for some root beer and a snack?"

"Yeah." Then he laughed and started recounting the troll story.

As we walked toward the woods, I heard the pop-pop-pop of Rick's tractor headed our way. Since we'd been gone so long, Rick figured we were stuck. He drove out of the woods toward us, stopped, and idled down the engine. I told him where Eric was, and Gabe and I trudged on to the fire pit. A few minutes later, we walked up on Tom, Sheila, and Francis standing around the fire and filled them in on the night's shenanigans. Gabe grabbed a root beer and a bag of chips. I stood at the fire for a few minutes, until Francis and I decided to walk back down to see if we could help. I made sure Gabe was warm and well supplied with kid beer and food and that Sheila and Tom would stay with him until I got back. Francis and I set off for what would become a comedy of errors.

We were slipping down the hill toward the finger of forest separating the fields and lamenting the booze we weren't consuming when I noticed three separate sets of lights below us: the Ranger, the tractor, and the drill rig. "Oh, shit," I said, "Rick got the tractor stuck." Sure enough, when we walked through the woods to the ditch that bordered the field above the Ranger, Rick stood beside his tractor, cursing. I saw that the rear blade he used for pushing snow had caught one side of the ditch as he drove through it, stranding the rear tires an inch or two off the ground. He couldn't raise the blade any further, and the tires couldn't get traction, so the tractor was stuck. I laughed, and said to Francis, "This is turning hilarious."

Things moved from hilarious to absurd. We tried to push the tractor out. Dumb. Eventually, we freed the tractor when Rick detached the blade by pounding the pins out with an anchor shackle. Rick drove down to the Ranger, pulled it out, and got the tractor stuck again. Eric buried the Ranger in another swale trying to get back to the tractor. We dug snow from around it and pushed it out. Then Eric pulled the tractor out. Both pieces of equipment freed, Francis and I jumped on the Ranger, Eric high-tailed it out to Ikes Road and then motored back to the fire pit via dirt roads, arriving about 3 a.m. I must have burned more calories digging in and walking through the snow than I do on a fifty-mile bike ride. Since I hadn't tasted any beer or bourbon in several hours, I told Gabe we'd be heading home soon—on the main roads this time. I'd had enough of stuck vehicles. Around the fire, we recounted our heroic deeds to watch $100 bills shooting out of the ground one more time, laughing at the absurdity of it. Gabe and I left the fire around 4:00 a.m.

I thought Gabe might go to sleep on the way home. Instead, during the fifteen-minute ride home, I heard the troll story three times, each punctuated by his belly laugh. We crept into the house, trying not to wake anyone up. I hustled him off to bed and fell into bed myself, smelling of smoke and thinking *that was ridiculous. The Redneck Pastoral. Awesome.*

—•—

I woke up thinking about coffee and the rig towering above our antics in the field, how the rig represented something huge, an energy and technology revolution, while we, a small group of partiers wallowing in the snow at its base represented what . . . the community? The place? We were apart from the industry yet also somehow a part of it. In the light of day, the well pad seemed simultaneously too close and too far away, a single rig and a symbol for a vast system. The rig drew us to it with the promise of seeing $100 bills shooting out of the ground, even though it stood impersonal and impenetrable while we tried to free our machines. If it hadn't been there, we would have stayed around the fire, I would have drunk more bourbon, and Gabe and I would have slept in the Man Hut. The rig had a presence that gave me a sense of being watched, even though we were on private property and were doing nothing wrong. We were stuck in the industry the same way we were stuck in the snow, but we couldn't dig ourselves out of the industry. We were having our fun, celebrating a memorable birthday, but that rig left its stamp on the proceedings.

I ground coffee beans and thought about those lovers in James Cameron's *Titanic*. Our silliness reminded me of the unlikely affair Leonardo DiCaprio and Kate Winslet's characters have in the midst of a massive tragedy-in-waiting. They were living their lives when the ship hit the iceberg. At Eric's party, we were living our lives in the midst of a huge drama playing itself out around us over hundreds of square miles—perhaps, depending on which way the drill bit pointed, even right below us. We could have been wrestling with stuck machines directly above a drill bore. Or the drill bit could have been chewing its way along under the fire pit. Cameron's lovers' story takes place against the historical backdrop of a disaster and, while the lovers and the movie-goers see their story as central, it's dwarfed by the larger story of the hubris that sank the ship. Thinking back over the previous night, I saw my life as very small compared to the industry. Thankfully, we wouldn't hit an actual iceberg, but who knew when something irreversible might happen, like a polluted water well? That night's craziness a short walk from the well pad drew in stark relief the extent to which Lilace and I were acting in our daily dramas while the industry chugged around us and beneath us, carrying us into an uncertain future. That's part of the problem with the industry. We know where it is, but we don't know where it's going.

—◦—

While we were out goofing off in the snow, people suffered in Dimock. Or so I found out via updates from my colleague, Kristin Sanner, who lived out that way. One day between classes, I saw Kristin's open office door and popped in to ask her how things were going. Kristin and her family lived in the country near Montrose, Pennsylvania, about two hours east of Whitneyville. Kristin and her husband taught, raised chickens, made maple syrup, and thought deeply about environmental issues. Like us, they refused to lease their land.

It didn't take long for our conversation to turn to natural gas. Kristin asked me if I had heard the latest about Dimock. When I shook my head, Kristin explained that Pennsylvania's Department of Environmental Protection (DEP) told the residents of Dimock that it was going to run a water line out to the residents from Scranton, about eight miles away. The water line would provide clean water to homeowners whose wells had been contaminated. Cabot agreed to help pay for the costs. However, according to Kristin, some locals who had benefited from the industry, or expected to, opposed spending the money on the water-line construction. One of the most vocal, a local businessman who sat on a conservancy board with Kristin and her husband, claimed that he was not willing to spend DEP's money to take care of the problems of a few people. I was aghast that someone could act so selfishly toward a group of people who had suffered due to a gas company's mistakes. Kristin explained, "This asshole wants to lease the conservancy land as well. Bill and I have been fighting him nonstop." I shook my head, not knowing what to say, yet recognizing that these kinds of dramas must play out wherever extractive industries drill. It's as though the drill rigs extract the sense of community from a place and pipe it away with the gas. Though it's not the case with all people—in many ways the gas industry pushed people together who may not have otherwise recognized their shared interests—the industry's arrival fracked our communities as well as the shale.

Hearing stories like Kristin's baffled me. And they kept adding up.

—◦—

A few months after Eric's party, Lilace came home from taking a photo of Shell Appalachia's office and told me about a house over on Ikes Road being bought by Shell. She said, "I was out taking a picture from the parking lot next door when a couple walked up to me and asked me what I was doing. I thought I was going to get run off, but when they found out what I was up to, they gave me their blessing. I asked if they'd had problems with the industry. The woman said 'We can't tell you, because we signed a nondisclosure agreement.' They wished me luck and left."

Turns out the house was just down the hill from the Vandergrift 290 well pad where we watched $100 bills shooting out of the ground. I asked Eric about it. He told me that Shell bought Jerry Gee's house because the water got trashed. He didn't know much more, but now I had a name so I could do some research. What I read scared me.

In the *Williamsport Sun-Gazette*, Cheryl Clarke (2011) reported that the Gees' pond and well water had been polluted by Shell's drilling activity. I read that the water "turned white" due to tiny gas bubbles filling it. The Gees experienced a frog and salamander die-off in their pond, which, according to water tests performed pre-drilling, was pristine. According to the DEP, the cause was a faulty casing around the drill bore, which resulted in thermogenic methane migrating into the Gees' water. While the Gees were assured that no other chemicals were present in their water supply, Shell acknowledged that other chemicals could make their way through the same fissures into the Gees' water. Shell took several steps to mitigate the problem, including supplying water buffaloes for drinking water, installing a methane detection device in the Gees' house, and putting fracking activities on hold. That Shell did not deny that its work caused the problem surprised me. But knowing that its fracking operation trashed the Gees' water provided positive proof that I was not overreacting when I voiced my concerns about our water being ruined. I mean, holy shit! Their house was a five-mile bike ride away, about three miles as the crow flies.

I had ridden by the Gees' house maybe fifty times. Ikes Road is one of the main connectors from Mansfield and Whitneyville to the dirt roads of Asaph. Mostly I rode that way to avoid traffic, though I liked to climb Ikes Road. It is one of the few hills around here that I can climb quickly when I'm in shape. I gleefully remember dropping the little troll, Tom, on this climb near the end of a fifty-four-mile training ride, the only time in nine years I've been able to do so. I have good memories of this road, even though most trips up it have been painful.

Clark's article also mentioned that the Gees had lived on their property for several generations. That caused another kind of pain for me. I tried to imagine how devastating it would feel to have the water at the Whitney house polluted, and we'd lived there less than a year. How could companies get away with this? How could a company compensate a family for wrecking their *home*?

—○—

On the Monday before Thanksgiving in 2011, I was riding my single-speed home from a busy morning at the university. The semester was winding down, or winding up, depending on your view, and I had been responding to student papers all morning. I was zoning out, thinking about meeting my son when he got off the bus, the paper-grading crunch that always happened at the end of the semester, and smoking a turkey with Dan Thanksgiving eve. I wasn't thinking about riding my bike.

I turned right off Lambs Creek Road onto Ore Bed Road, passed a well pad entrance, and pedaled steadily while looking south past the compressor stations on the next ridge. I looked north toward the stretch of forest where I usually saw a pileated woodpecker. No luck. I glanced at my watch. 3:15. Gabe got home at 3:35. I had five minutes to spare. I pedaled up a slight rise and dropped down a short grade . . .

. . . and found myself being helped toward a pickup truck by a stranger. I had crashed my bike, but I didn't remember how. I crawled in the backseat and gave the driver Lilace's phone number. We chatted. I have no idea about what, just that my lips moved, sounds came out, and I couldn't focus on anything.

An ambulance pulled up and EMTs brought a stretcher over to the truck. I think I said I didn't need it and walked to the ambulance. Around then, Lilace and our daughter showed up. I have an image of my daughter's concerned face etched into my mind, a flash of clarity in the otherwise continuous blur that had become my world. I think I told her I was okay. I think I said something to Lilace like "Can you get my bike?" or "Be sure to get my bike." Usually that's a sign the crasher is okay. Not this time.

I rode the ambulance to the hospital. I don't know what we did in the ambulance, except that I think I joked with the EMTs. About what, I have no idea. One EMT was a former student, but I wouldn't realize that until he told me in the hall at MU a couple of weeks later. I still don't remember seeing him. The EMTs rolled me into the hospital in Wellsboro and took me straight to x-ray. Turns out I had broken my collarbone and three ribs. Then the pain kicked in. A nurse asked me if I wanted to try to take my jersey off, since jerseys were expensive. I said, "Cut it off." Uttering that phrase told me I was seriously fucked up.

I got a CT scan—an excruciating ordeal with the broken ribs. I don't know what they saw, but the doctor said I had a pretty bad concussion. The nurse pumped me full of pain meds, and Lilace's priest showed up. I laid on the ER bed and forgot everything I said.

Eventually the doctor decided I could leave. I slid my legs off the bed and, with Lilace's and a nurse's help, stood up to move to a wheelchair. Bad move. My peripheral vision squeezed in until I could only see what was right in front of my face and all the voices sounded like they were under water. "I've gotta sit down," I said, easing back onto the bed.

"Do you need something else for the pain?" the doctor asked.

"Yes." He gave me another shot. I stretched out for a few minutes until whatever it was (Demerol? Dilaudid?) kicked in and I could make it to the wheelchair. Lilace drove us to pick up the kids and then home. I remember next to nothing.

I learned later that I was lying unconscious in the road when a retired MU policeman and his wife stopped to help me. I had a Grade II concussion and a collarbone that required ten screws, a steel plate, and cadaver bone (thanks—whomever you were) to repair. The surgeon said my collarbone was "powder." After the accident I never had headaches and couldn't feel the collarbone break, but the broken ribs kept me washing Vicodin and Percocet down with beer for days. Probably the scariest thing was my short-term memory was gone. That made it hard to respond to student papers, but I managed by taking lots of notes. I also looked at the cracks in my helmet every so often. Without that thing, well. My crash would have been really bad.

—◦—

At some point in the ER I remembered what happened, though it's hazy to this day. Lilace said I told her, "I hit a hole. Wasn't paying attention, just hurrying downhill, didn't have my hands wrapped around the grips. They bounced off and underneath the handlebars. I don't remember anything after that. Damn rookie mistake." Later Lilace told me she was sure I'd been hit by a gas truck. Not so. I screwed up all by myself. I was so distracted by all the stuff going on—the end of the semester, the university's shaky finances, the gas boom, the constant worry and stress—that I forgot to ride my bike. Distracted, I was numb to what I was actually doing at the moment. And I paid.

Nothing good is without risk. Riding bikes, climbing rocks, teaching classes, getting married, having kids, buying a house—all of these involve risk. Playing outside has taught me I always have to weigh the risks against the rewards, and I have to recognize I can't control every single moment. I wear a helmet for that reason. Thank Gaia. I want to ride bikes with my kids. Hug my wife. Teach more classes. Drink more beer. Make more noise.

7 Flowback

⌗ "Hey, Obama, we don't need no fracking drama! Hey, Obama, we don't need no fracking drama!" The chant rolled across the West Lawn of the Capitol in DC as Lilace and I walked up through a sweltering July day in 2012 to join the Stop the Frack Attack Rally. Stop the Frack Attack was a protest organized by grassroots activists affected by gas drilling, and it has spawned into an activist group with a wide reach, including my home state of North Carolina.[1] People traveled from all over the United States and Australia to protest the natural gas industry. Speakers included author Bill McKibben, Josh Fox of *Gasland* fame, some teenagers from West Virginia and Pennsylvania, a Native American from the Blackfeet Nation in Montana, and Pittsburgh politician Doug Shields. A bluegrass band called Stick Mob kept people entertained between speeches. I was struck by the mishmash of people that made up the crowd: aging hippies, grandmas and grandpas, middle-aged white- and blue-collar workers, soon-to-be aging hippies, babies and toddlers, teens, people flying solo, and people in groups. Many races were represented, though whites predominated. I felt like I had been dropped into the melting pot, which warmed my heart.

I was also sweating more than usual, due partly to the heat and partly to the fact I am not comfortable at big protests. I've been to a few, and I believe that such protests can bring attention to issues that need it, but I prefer to stay at home and lob my complaints in writing from afar. My discomfort did not stop me from grabbing a Stop the Frack Attack sign when I was offered one, so I could participate as fully as possible in what I saw as a giant rhetorical act.

At first I was disappointed in the size of the crowd. It just didn't seem that big, given the reach of the gas industry and the wreaking of havoc on communities. Where the hell was everyone? I wanted to fill the mall all the way down to the Washington Monument. Of course pedaling the sacrifice zone meant that fracking was a lens through which I viewed almost everything. In 2012 it boggled my mind when I went to places where drilling wasn't occurring and talked with people who had never heard of it.

When Stop the Frack Attack protestors gathered to start our march to deliver jugs of polluted well water to the American Petroleum Institute and the American Natural Gas Alliance about a mile and a half away, the crowd grew in size until I felt this was a proper protest. We started up Pennsylvania Avenue and covered almost three city blocks. The next day, I read estimates of 5,000 chanting, marching people.[2] Not awesome, by any means, but a hell of a lot bigger than other protests I've been to. And I've got to admit that the more we walked, the more hopeful I felt, not because we were going to change anyone's mind that day or that the president would call an emergency press conference to enact a drilling moratorium that evening, but because here was a group of people who cared enough to come together and create one big symbolic act in order to make their voices heard. The rally in DC came to stand for me as a coalescing of a multitude of smaller, individual voices that had begun protesting the industry's work several years earlier.

—◦—

When I began researching the gas industry in 2008 and 2009, I became concerned at the lack of voices offering up a perspective that differed from the industry's economic and patriotic one. I heard from individuals here and there who questioned the industry, yet there seemed to be no overarching message or cohesive voice like that of the gas industry. This changed over time as I discovered bloggers who questioned the industry, documented the impacts, and called for decisions based on something other than economics. Some of these blogs were *Ada Mae Compton, Tioga County, PA Gas Watch, How Should We Do the Mountain, The Faces of Frackland, Honesdale Concerned Citizens, Shaleshock,* TXSharon's *Bluedaze,* and others. There was our blog, *Greetings from Pipeline Road 7,* which helped Lilace and me connect with others and channel stress. As residents who lived above the shale, the bloggers questioned the gas industry's message, and they provided a clearinghouse of information on all kinds of things, including up-to-date information on laws, protests, politicians' stances, drilling accidents, insurance issues, and personal experiences with the industry. These blogs represented deeply concerned citizens and helped fill any gaps I had in my knowledge about the industry's work in the Marcellus and elsewhere. The blogs marked the beginning of a larger response to the industry, one that gained force as people learned more about the industry.

Another source that influenced the way I saw the public's response to the gas industry's rhetoric came from a Google group called Citizens Concerned about Natural Gas Drilling (CCNGD). CCNGD described itself as a "nonpartisan group of citizens concerned with the potential negative social, environmental, and economic impacts of natural gas drilling development in Tioga County, PA," putting them in direct opposition to MSC's positive message. The group was created in October 2009, grew to over 200 members, and is still going strong, keeping people abreast of the latest information about gas development, upcoming public meetings, plans for protests, deadlines for public comment, and the like. Members shared emails with subject lines like "Dumping Well Site Soil behind Wysox Kiln Mill along River Bank," "Urge EPA to Increase Public Participation in Natural

Gas Decisions," and "How Natural Gas Development is Affecting Forestland [*sic*]." The information provided members with a sense of community and brought people together who might otherwise not have connected. Perhaps most important, for me anyway, the Google group created a virtual community of like-minded people who questioned the industry's story and provided alternative stories for the future. Knowing that I wasn't the only one with the questions I saw asked by members of CCNGD lent weight to my perspective and encouraged me to keep it up.

—◦—

In *Publics and Counterpublics*, Michael Warner explains that, in order for a public or counterpublic to be created, it must be written (or spoken) into existence (2002, 67). The industry wrote one version of a public into existence, an idea of a public defined by a bright economic future and patriotic sacrifice. Locals concerned about gas development encountered this frame when they sought information that offered alternative visions, visions based on clean air and water and a quiet, rural life. Not all locals questioned the industry, but those who did found conflicting or contradictory information that undermined the industry's rosy projections. Made up of environmentalists, disgruntled landowners, and others, local citizens told their stories, partially disrupting the stories told by the industry. That was part of the goal for our blog. While locals did not have the PR funds or professionals enjoyed by the industry, they formed a counterpublic that challenged the gas industry's notion that northcentral Pennsylvania was simply a resource to be exploited. Providing an important imaginative grounding, stories told by locals to locals and outsiders populated the region with flesh-and-blood humans invested in the place. The same flesh-and-blood humans who shouted and sweated in DC.

Like the industry, northcentral Pennsylvanians used multiple media to create a sense of themselves as a public and pushed back against the industry's vision for the future. The locals' message grew in part from its rootedness in the place, not the resource, and it competed with the message of locals who for various reasons supported the industry at the expense of the place. These locals' rhetorical acts invited the "pause in movement" Tuan claims is so crucial to creating a sense of place (1977, 138). Once this pause in movement occurred, the momentum of the industry was blunted, because the audience was invited to pause and think of north-central Pennsylvania as something other than a resource.

It may be too late to change completely the industry's economic frame, but it's not too late to talk about—and work toward—alternative futures. We see potential for change in the way Chesapeake's "This Is Our Home" ads aligned the company with locals' concerns and attempted to define the future in terms broader than economic. Though not perfect, hearing locals' voices and seeing the industry's response is a hell of a lot better that MSC's gloss of "positive impacts."

—○—

Back when I recounted my experiences processing turkeys with Mike Chester, I talked about the importance of putting theory into practice. That's what this book is—theory into practice. I have tried to represent part of my life in ways that show how theories of rhetoric have made their way into every fiber of my being. Why? Because in this day and age of symbols flying all over the place, it matters. We have to learn how to negotiate these symbols in order to avoid the kinds of problems that plague us, like a lack of action on climate change or short-sighted education reform or the abuse of communities by extractive industries. While it's arguable that understanding how language functions in our complicated world may not help us immediately or even in all cases, there's no way we can fight for a world that we want without understanding how to use language in ways that promote our own agendas. Yes, I said agendas, because that's what we argue for. In meetings, we can't "win" all the time. But we need language to join our agendas, items, concerns, and issues with other, like-minded agendas, to form alliances, to give our words more weight. There's no way we can take any kind of meaningful action or make any kind of meaningful change without understanding how rhetoric plays a role. As Kenneth Burke suggests, "The *confinements* of the road are also the conditions of its *freedom*" (1966, 472). And even when there's no traffic, sometimes you hit a pothole and fall on your head. And sometimes you find yourself in a huge clusterfuck you didn't see coming.

—◦—

Paul Wendel's email appeared in my inbox on December 8, 2013, a little over a month after I came off the latest retrenchment list. A former colleague at Mansfield University and co-founder of the Mansfield Growers Market, Paul was on the 2010 MU retrenchment list and had taken a position at Otterbein University in Ohio. Lilace and I remained close with Paul and his wife, Joyce, and we enjoyed those times together, rare now that they had moved, when we drank bourbon and ate chocolate while chatting about kids, food, cycling, politics, and the university. In his email, Paul asked for a place to crash, since he and two colleagues from MU were presenting preliminary results from their ongoing study called "The Effects of Natural Gas Drilling on Groundwater Quality in Tioga County, PA" in Wellsboro. He promised to bring some Bailey's; I couldn't say no. I looked forward to seeing his presentation, which we had discussed before, in more detail.

The next day I checked my Yahoo! email account for my daily fix of natural gas news from the CCNGD listserv, my Marcellus

Alerts list, and the Gas Business Briefing website. To my surprise and dismay, I saw a subject line from a friend at CCNGD, John Kesich, which read "Wendel—propaganda masquerading as science." I opened the message and read the first line: "Sadly. [*sic*] Pine Creek Headwaters Protection Group has decided to sponsor a presentation by Dr. Paul Wendel and two of his coauthors. They claim, 'the [study's] findings indicate only a modest impact on water quality [from fracking].'" The email questioned Paul's "research"—yes, research appeared in quotes—and encouraged people who had been affected by the industry to attend and let Paul know how "modest" gas drilling impacts were. The email included a link to John's website. John's site contained the questions about Paul's research that John had sent to two scientists, the co-sponsors of the public forum, Pine Creek Headwaters Protection Group, and the Northcentral Pennsylvania Conservancy, and a letter he had mailed to Paul detailing his questions. I read the first line: "This study seems seriously flawed, maybe even outright propaganda." *What the fuck?* I thought. *Paul's a propagandist? What the fuck is your problem, John?* Propaganda involves a concerted effort and message by a group or organization designed to provoke a certain outcome. Propaganda starts with answers, not questions. Paul may not have provided the answers John or I wanted, but it began from questions Paul and his collaborators wanted to answer, not with answers already in mind.

As I read further, I noticed that John had many of the same questions I did about the study, including a concern about the possibility that the study might in some way endorse the gas industry. But the idea that Paul was a propagandist offended me, and I stewed in my office for most of the morning, wondering if I should send a rebuttal. It's one thing to question research; it's another to question someone's character. I decided to keep my mouth shut. Paul and I are friends. Paul's a bike-riding, Prius-driving environmentalist but wouldn't screw up his science cred to meet an agenda. I also appreciate tremendously the amount of environmental and political activism John takes on in Tioga County. We were both at the Stop the Frack Attack Rally in DC. But I couldn't square John's reaction with what I knew of Paul.

Paul arrived about an hour before his presentation and changed into his suit and tie, then we headed over to the Toyishi Center so he could get his PowerPoint presentation fired up. On the drive over, I mentioned John's CCNGD email, and Paul said that he'd read it. He added that a co-researcher had researched John's website, and they'd decided not to send their research to John, mainly because they weren't sure how it would be used. Paul added that they had been receiving helpful feedback at conferences, and they were drafting an article for peer review.

As Paul drove into the parking lot of the Toyishi Center, I spotted John's distinctive profile beside the entrance. We hopped out of the car and walked over to the door; as John gave us a handout he had prepared, I introduced him to Paul. They shook hands, and Paul thanked John for coming. We left John and made our way to the conference room. I gave John's handout a cursory glance. Single-spaced text covered both sides, and the handout appeared to be a summary of what John had posted on his website. I tucked it in the back of my journal and wondered what John's opinion would be at the end of the presentation.

In the Toyishi Training Center's conference room, the Pine Creek Headwaters Protection Group's monthly meeting was in progress at a table in the back. A woman with long brown hair excused herself from the group and walked over. Reneé Carey introduced herself as the executive director of the Northcentral Pennsylvania Conservancy and showed Paul where he would be setting up his slide show. While they fiddled with cables, I surveyed the room and saw Jim Weaver, Tioga County planner, sitting at the table. I recognized a couple of faces I had seen at other public forums on natural gas. As Paul finished hooking up his computer and tested his slideshow, Reneé and I chatted about her work, tonight's attendance, and retrenchment at MU. People streamed in behind us, crowding around the coffee pot and donuts in the back of the room, shaking hands, and making their way toward seats. I sat in the back and watched County Commissioner Roger Bunn take a seat in front of me. *Far out, Paul*, I thought. *You've drawn out the big guns.*

While a slide behind them displayed "The Effect of Natural Gas Drilling on Groundwater Quality in Tioga, PA," Reneé introduced Paul, Dr. Shaker Ramasamy, an MU chemistry professor, and Andy Ford, an MU chemistry graduate, as co-researchers on the project and turned the floor over to Paul. Paul offered a brief description of their research question on how drilling was affecting water in Tioga County and then launched into a review of natural gas drilling and a thorough overview of the research process, including the design. He described how the researchers cobbled together money and sent Andy Ford and other students around the county to collect water samples from places that met the project's criteria, how they worked assiduously to avoid any possibility of human bias creeping into the water testing itself, and how they lost a few volunteers between Phase I and Phase II of collecting water samples. Paul walked around the front of the room, referring to slides and reciting numbers, yet he seemed uncharacteristically nervous in front of the crowd and frequently struggled for words. I didn't blame him. From our earlier talks, I suspected many people would not be happy with his research, because it did not show as definitively as people might hope that gas drilling caused widespread problems with groundwater. So far John's response had been the most vocal example, but Paul was opening up the study to wider criticism this night.

Paul covered a tremendous amount of statistical terminology over the course of forty minutes, most of it baffling me. He talked of "t tests," "standard deviations," "variance," "double-blind tests," and a host of other statistical methods, the purpose of which was to ensure objectivity. I'm no statistician, but I found the sheer amount of work the researchers did to eliminate human bias somewhat comforting, especially since much of what I read about natural gas drilling contained clear bias. Perhaps the most interesting fact to me came when Paul stated that the aquifer in Tioga County is relatively shallow, which means that the water flows faster and replenishes more often than a deep aquifer. I wasn't sure what that could mean for our water, but it reminded me of geography professor Chris Kopf telling me that all the water in Tioga County goes somewhere else. The most alarming thing I took away from Paul's presentation was that conductivity is higher and more strontium is present in water wells tested within 400 meters of a fracked well.[3] These results suggest that fracking does affect the groundwater, though Paul termed the effects "modest."

Paul wrapped up his presentation and turned the floor back to Reneé, who asked for questions. Hands shot up. Reneé pointed to a gentleman sitting in front of me wearing a brown suit coat, a tie, wire-rimmed glasses, and unruly gray hair. He leaned forward. "Thanks for your presentation, Paul," the man said. "I'm Ed Osgood, and we've heard all this talk about safe, clean natural gas. So, I've got a question for you. Can you say it's safe?"

Paul hesitated a moment and said, "No." The man leaned back. "But," Paul added, "I can't say that it's not safe either."

He looked at Reneé, who called on Bryn Hammerstrom, a local I recognized from other natural gas meetings. Balding with a gray ponytail, Bryn frequently writes for the local newspaper about the gas industry and other political concerns. Tonight, he focused on the amount of activity occurring in the ground with the drilling and fracking. He mentioned the Gee family receiving a $750,000 buyout from Shell when the water on their property was polluted. His statement surprised me. I knew Shell had bought it, but I didn't know for how much. Since the Gees signed a nondisclosure agreement, they can't talk about it. Coming to his question, Bryn asked Paul if he had any idea how much the groundwater would be affected by all the activity. Paul said he didn't know. Then John asked a question about whether Paul's study could "clarify that the actual concrete was leaking." He was referring to a study that claimed between 2 and 6 percent of all well casings leaked from the outset of drilling (see Ingraffea 2013). Paul said that was outside the scope of their study. Questions continued, mostly about specific cases that resulted in groundwater pollution from spills or failed casings.

Over the course of the questions, I saw that Paul's research was driven by his positivist perspective, what he and his co-researchers could observe, while the audience's concerns were driven by what they had observed plus other worries. Paul's research worked in terms of abstractions and statistical analysis; audience members mentioned families who had been affected, specifically the Gees and the Johnsons, the latter a family who lost cows when a holding pond filled with flowback water collapsed. One question came up repeatedly about what would happen to the water twenty or thirty years down the road. Paul admitted that he had no answer, but he and Dr. Ramasamy spoke to the importance of continuing this kind of research in order to keep tabs on drilling's effects on groundwater. I found myself torn. On the one hand, living as close as I did to several fracked wells, I worried about how my water might be affected. On the other, Paul's research and the audience's questions drove home to me that we often focus on the homes adversely affected by drilling and overlook the houses that are affected minimally or not at all. There is risk in most things. Discovering how much and deciding if it's worth it is our job. Paul's research helped.

Though I shared concerns with the audience, especially about the long-range consequences for our water, I also felt a bit of psychic breathing space, as though the wells had moved a few hundred yards further from our house. This was no about-face on my part. I still distrust the industry, and the Gees' and Johnsons' stories are just two of a long list of people affected negatively by drilling. I know, too, that Paul has his own reservations about the industry, which is why he and his co-researchers bent over backward to eliminate human bias.

Paul's research provided another result for me that had little to do with his research question. It involved the language we use when we talk about natural gas and how we are inclined to see things from our own agendas. Paul's research pulled me in different directions and pushed me to think more carefully about others' attitudes compared to my own. Paul is a trusted friend, and, honestly, I wanted him to find results stronger than "modest." I checked the dictionary to try to gauge whether Paul had chosen the best word. "Modest" is defined as "moderate in size or amount," which seemed fair to characterize his findings. I would have preferred he found results "off the charts" or "Holy shit, there's a lot of crap in the water!" (as long as it wasn't my water). Paul's allegiance is to science, and his picture could be used alongside another definition of "modest": "not vain, not boasting about one's merits or achievements." His results, however much I disliked them, gave me a bit more peace of mind. I was still torn and distrustful but also a little relieved.

John's reaction told a different story. John had run for county commissioner in the past, and I voted for him, because he and I shared concerns about the environment. In this instance, however, I found myself cringing at John's preemptive discrediting of Paul's work as "propaganda." That hardly seemed fair, given that Paul and his co-researchers were trying to establish some understanding of how gas drilling affected groundwater around here. John was coming from the right place (according to my agenda), which is why I voted for him, and he frames many issues in terms of climate change, same as me. His initial reaction to Paul's research was not modest but self-righteous and accusatory, a reaction more divisive than helpful when it comes to rhetoric. In a follow-up email to CCNGD from December 22, John's opinion did not appear to have changed much. He began his email by stating, "I can't help but wonder how ethical it is to present the conclusions of a study that relies on convoluted statistical analysis to the general public before it has been peer reviewed; Wendel admitted he has yet to publish at his 12/18 presentation." John continued, "The presentation went pretty much as I expected; except I kept expecting him to say, 'trust me, I'm a scientist.'" This line is about the only place John cut Paul any slack. Otherwise, I read phrases like the following:

- "One thing he couldn't wish away was an increase in strontium between Phase I and Phase II; he said the increase was small and it wasn't clear if it was something to worry about. That must be alright then; in fact, down-right encouraging. . . ."
- "The issue of nondisclosure agreements came up, as did the question of whether true impacts might not show up for '30 years.' Wendel said nothing worth hearing on either point. He did say that further study was necessary and also pointed out that funding is tight."
- "As I feared, the real propaganda coup came in the form of [the newspaper article "Speaker: Study of Water Wells Near Gas Drilling Is Encouraging"; Clarke 2013]. At least the people attending the talk had the benefit of some questions and hearing Wendel admit 'I don't know,'

'We didn't look at that' and the like. People reading that
Williamsport rag will come away 'encouraged' that fracking is safe. I expect a similar item in next week's *Wellsboro
Gazette*. It is frustrating that Wendel is winning hearts
and minds while those who could knowledgeably
challenge his findings wait for a peer reviewed paper."
(As if Paul was running for office.)

John also characterized Paul's response to his question about
whether there should be a moratorium on new gas wells as "Wendel weaseled out of answering by saying he assumed those were
rhetorical questions."

Apparently, John felt that Paul's research efforts provided nothing useful in terms of the knowledge about the gas industry. John
jumped to conclusions—if it's not clear that strontium levels are
bad, then they must be "alright"—and used words like "convoluted," "weaseled," "rhetorical,"[4] and "winning hearts and minds"
to shape the way people on the CCNGD listserv understood
Paul's presentation. John wanted it both ways. He dismissed the
science because it didn't agree with his view, saying Paul and his
collaborators were claiming unearned authority. But when Paul
wouldn't weigh in on something that hadn't been studied, choosing not to claim authority until studies showed something, he was,
in John's eyes, dodgy and weaseling.

I found myself angered by John's rhetoric for the way it attacked
someone who shared his concerns and who once called this place
home. John's framing seemed counterproductive to me, and it
made me question John's attitude, though we race for the same
team. I wanted to distance myself from him, because I understood Paul's work to support the very concerns that so engage, and
enrage, John but that also seemed counterproductive. As I showed
earlier, the industry provides a coordinated message that works in

its favor, and environmentalists need to challenge other greens acting in bad faith. But pointing a finger at any study that does not support your agenda 100 percent is a bad thing. It fractures communities.

Part of John's response stemmed from his concern that the industry was moving too fast and the science too slow. I agree. We know too little about the industry's long-range impacts to let it drill like crazy. But the industry's economic framing tends to garner support for its work, especially in a depressed economy. And, unfortunately, extractive industries don't *have* to proceed at the same pace as science. Paul's research took time, and many wells were drilled while he and his colleagues collected water samples and analyzed them. The industry worries less about questions driving Paul's research than about moving quickly to maximize profit. The speed with which the industry invaded this place carries with it an inherent advantage, too, in the sense that when researchers like Paul or the Cornell professors show research that casts doubts on whether natural gas drilling is clean, the industry can say, "But we've always done it this way." It's more difficult to stop a bike once it's rolling. So I get John's animosity toward and distrust of Paul, though I think it's misguided.

This kind of distrust runs deep. When I mentioned to my friend Randy, whose family had lost a lot due to the industry, in spring 2013 that I had been invited to join the advisory board for MU's Marcellus Institute, he stared at me a moment, looked down, and stated flatly that he could never do that, because it was a "frackademic group." I understood his response—if anyone should have a negative opinion of the gas industry, it's Randy and his family—and I worried that my presence on the advisory board would appear as though I support natural gas drilling without question. That's not the case. I have a track record of questioning the industry through my blog, at regional and national conferences, in newspapers and academic essays, in on-campus presentations, and in this book. I agreed to serve on the Marcellus Institute Advisory Board because I wanted to hear what people at the university were thinking about natural gas development and what sort of public message the university put forth regarding it. There are times when changes can be made from inside an institution, and I looked at my role on the board as one of asking hard questions and calling bullshit when needed. I couldn't try to shape the Institute's message about natural gas from the outside. But Randy's family lost much due to an industry screw-up, and that weighed on me even as Paul's research gave me some mental breathing room. I got Randy's reaction, and I hoped that he didn't see me as a turncoat.

What I find most bothersome about the tension I encounter during such experiences is the way it affects my perception of the place. The forests don't hold the promise they once did. I think part of the reason for this change in perception has to do with the way Paul's, John's, Randy's, and my perspectives all tie closely into how we see and use this land. Even though we're working for the same outcomes, the tensions I perceive between us caused by our respective experiences of the industry threaten to divide us. The land suffers for that.

I value knowing Paul, John, and Randy. I like them, and I need to hear their perspectives. We don't agree on everything, nor do I expect us to. We are each working to create a better world for ourselves and others, one that is about more than trashing a place by drilling for gas. Yet in small ways we're pitted against each other, which takes energy we could aim at the gas industry.

—o—

My sense of this place has been altered by my experiences with the industry. I don't mind more people coming here, or who they are, and I don't mind people making money, but I worry that the land and the water and the health of this place will be sacrificed to power energy–hungry homes and industry, the same way West Virginia's mountaintops have been. I worry about fractured relationships, perhaps the most effective way to trash a place.

When I first began rooting into this place, I felt memories and land commingled in intimate ways. Now I look at the land differently, more abstractly. Instead of sinking roots further into the ground, there's a sense that my life is being played out on a stage controlled by industry. My romantic sense of place, in all its Wordsworthian glory, clashes with the industrial work it so desperately wants to remain apart from. I've learned this place well over the past nine years, and I learn more about it every day. Even with the insecurity and unrest that blankets this area, the good still outweighs the bad. But I am the sum of my past and all my experiences, much of which involves the study of environmental issues, and I can't help but begin to feel a distrust of the land that shapes my legs, lungs, and heart. It's subtle, but it's here, in my mind and memory. Most saddening to me is that this distrust is not this place's fault—I have good memories—but the fault of the extractive industry. I mean, I am living in my favorite house ever. How do I reconcile those feelings?

It's as if a place that I once saw as containing endless possibilities now offers fewer. I've never experienced this feeling before. It's striking and a little frightening, a growing foreboding. On rides, I look out at the mountains rolling away to all sides, and they seem a little dryer, a little more brittle. This is odd, given that the land around here has shown itself to be remarkably resilient, having bounced back from the destructive industries of tanning, logging, and coal mining. But I still see the signs, at least of the mining— the river running through Mansfield is basically dead. Lessons from the past do not take hold around here.

Maybe what I'm experiencing is a nagging doubt that this time the land won't bounce back. It pains me to say that. I have great faith in nature and natural processes, and I'm astounded at what an ecosystem, left to its own devices, can do. And maybe as a part of this worry I see a time when my family may not bounce back from whatever the future holds for us as we grow alongside the gas industry. These thoughts contribute to my sense of this place.

And remind me of a ride home. On my usual commute on Ore Bed Road, I remember pedaling and looking south toward Arnot as I crested Ore Bed's highest point. The sun was shining, a slight breeze rustled the trees, and clouds meandered across the sky, casting shadows on the fields and forests. The mountains rolled away into the distance, lending weight to the name "Endless Mountains." Every time I see this view from this spot, I think of Nevada's deserts and the way I could see for miles out there. On this ride, though, the mountains looked brittle, like they could crumble, even though I couldn't see any drill rigs or gas trucks. Nothing had changed that view, except that the industry had been here for a couple of years and I'd been living in the whirl of words that came with it. I turned my attention back to the road as I descended into the small valley that marks the last couple of miles before home. The wind whistled through my helmet, my tires crunched the gravel, and I steered around potholes at close to 40 mph. The speed couldn't blow away my realization that the way I saw the land had changed.

I cranked up the final grade to the house, out of sorts, feeling like a mountain biker who thinks he knows where he is but the trail confuses him and his truck doesn't appear when he thinks it should. I pulled up to the garage, parked my bike, and grabbed a beer, hoping the suds would rinse my vibe away.

Epilogue

⌗   As I was working on this book at Madroño Ranch in Texas in November 2013, not far from the Barnett and Eagle Ford shale gas plays, I read two books: Richard Heinberg's (2013) *Snake Oil: How Fracking's False Promise of Plenty Imperils Our Future* and Gregory Zuckerman's (2013) *The Frackers: The Outrageous Inside Story of the New Billionaire Wildcatters*. A Senior Fellow at the Post Carbon Institute, Heinberg wrote a book that focuses on energy use and economics within a framework of climate change and challenges the industry's claim that there is as much natural gas as it says there is, and, anyway, we've got to cut our carbon consumption before the planet cuts it for us. Heinberg's book includes charts and graphs that show, among other things, the rise and decline of gas and oil production in various plays, and he places these fluctuations in the context of global energy. In his final section called "A Mirage Distracts Us from Hydrocarbon Rehab," Heinberg explains the complexity of our "energy-economy-climate situation" by making what he calls "two equally true statements":

- "Hydrocarbons are so abundant that, if we burn a substantial proportion of them, we risk a climate catastrophe beyond imagining."
- "There aren't enough economically accessible, high-quality hydrocarbons to maintain world economic growth for much longer." (2012, 123)

As Heinberg explains throughout his book, we have plenty of hydrocarbons in the ground. The problem is that, as we use up what people in the industry call "sweet spots," we find it increasingly difficult to access hydrocarbons. Heinberg cautions us to think carefully about the idea, claimed by the industry, that there are millions of cubic feet of natural gas waiting to be extracted. Heinberg suggests it's more complicated than that (also see Powers 2013).

An award-winning journalist who writes for *The Wall Street Journal*, Zuckerman tells the stories of "The Frackers," twenty-two oilmen and -women who play central roles in the twenty-first century's fracking boom. Zuckerman sees this as a drama, which it undoubtedly is, and provides a "Cast of Characters" on page ix, calling to mind Shakespeare or David Mamet. Whereas Heinberg's tone is somber, even worried, Zuckerman's tone is breathless with excitement: "The more work I put into the topic, the clearer it became that a burst of drilling in shale and other long-overlooked rock formations had created the biggest phenomenon to hit the business world since the housing and technology booms. In some ways, the impact of the energy bonanza might even be more dramatic than the previous expansions, especially if shale drilling catches on around the globe. Surging oil and gas production likely will affect governments, companies, and individuals in remarkable ways for decades to come" (2013, 2).

Like Heinberg, Zuckerman includes his own bulleted list. However, Zuckerman's list focuses on the large increase in oil and gas production in the United States; falling energy prices that benefit consumers, workers, and businesses; and the potential for boosting the US dollar and reducing the trade deficit (2013, 2–5). I thought it would be awesome if Zuckerman could channel some of those funds to MU's budget. For a fraction of the cash thrown around by the people Zuckerman followed, MU would be stable financially for years. No retrenchments!

Zuckerman's book was more exciting than Heinberg's, partly because they are not of the same genre. Heinberg's is polemical; Zuckerman's is biographical. Both draw on research but to different ends. The expertise of each author plays a role in the books as well.

Heinberg is an energy expert whose main job is to educate the public about the problems with touting an oil and gas boom when science suggests we need to cut back on hydrocarbon use. Zuckerman reports for a pro-business newspaper, and his bulleted list suggests that he favors business interests over others. In short, each writer's attitude toward his subject shapes his response to it. My attitude shapes my response to the books as well, and while I enjoyed Zuckerman's, I found it lacking in relevance to the issues we face today. Instead, I longed for a book written for a general audience that was dramatic and factually grounded and held drilling for natural gas up alongside climate change. But the problem with drama is that it can end up like Al Gore's CGI polar bears in *An Inconvenient Truth*—a way to dismiss complex arguments as much as a way to make them believable.

—◦—

I've pedaled over 25,000 miles since I moved to Tioga County. From all this riding, I learned more about who I am, who we are as humans, and what sort of world I want to live in. I've begun to understand that where I am—my place—is created in part by my physical experiences of the county. I've also learned that, no matter how much time I spend outside, most of what I know will come from symbols.

Riding a bike is like reading a book. I ride through Tioga State Forest at Asaph. Up, down, right, left, trees, meadows, creek crossings, log crossings, gravel roads, swoopy singletrack, deer, turkeys, grouse, the occasional bobcat or bear or hiker or truck. I encounter all sorts of stimuli that tweak the way I ride in that moment and that change me. When I finish a ride, I'm never the same person who started it. Likewise, when I read a book or essay or newspaper article or see a film, my perspective shifts, and I'm not the same.

I've realized that riding a bike is not merely a metaphor for reading but an act of reading a place. Like any book, there are limitations to what I learn while riding my bike. But pushing the pedals shapes the way I read my place, like the texts I've read do. Over the course of each ride, I pedal thousands of revolutions that adapt to the terrain—pedals resist going up, spin easily going down. My breathing deepens when my legs labor under the pressure of pushing up 10 percent grades and slows when I lose the elevation I gained. I read the landscape, choosing when to brake, when to accelerate, when to turn my head to follow five turkeys flying into the trees, where to stop and pluck an apple dangling from a branch, where potholes lurk that might send me or my compadres sliding down the asphalt or gravel, where I might spy a scarlet tanager when I fill my water bottles at the spring on Arnot Road. There's constant variation on the roads, calling to my mind the choices a good writer makes as she unrolls the words on the page like a ribbon of road or trail, the pace changing as the story builds suspense or plunges toward the climax. On the bike, I read through my eyes and legs and lungs, feet and hands and butt, and I learn about the shapes and contours of the land the way a book teaches me about the contours of living.

I'm a strong believer in commitment. Both cycling and reading show commitment to things like truth and knowledge. Though we don't have to ride bikes, we do have to read. Riding bikes has helped me commit to this place because I learned its geography, its moods, felt them in my body as I've shaped my perception of this place. I know the back roads, where red efts are most likely to hang out, when and where I'll probably see deer, and where the tartest apples grow. I read the landscape and at the same time I am inscribing my own story on the landscape. As I ride, I read the changes inscribed in the landscape by the gas industry—the huge swaths of trees and fields cleared for pipelines (many already buried and reseeded), well pads, holding ponds, compressor stations; orange extension cords snaking along the roads and plugged into yellow boxes for seismic testing; and even the new additions to houses, new cars and trucks, new roofs, new barns, new tractors, and new businesses.

Riding bikes inscribes the land into my body the way books inscribe ideas into my mind and the way the gas industry inscribes the landscape with pipeline right-of-ways and well pads. I'm invested in this place now, a place that literally shapes me and a place for which I feel responsible. The industry is invested as well, but in a different way. When it is done, it's done, like leaving a book unfinished or a bike outside in the rain.

That's no way to live.

—○—

We read our places through our physical experiences of them and through the symbols we encounter about them. The symbols we encounter and use suggest how we should use these places, too, whether to develop a natural resource, preserve state game lands, or protect our water or property. Sometimes all three. In that way, we take an active role in shaping the place, that is, how it is used. That's a weighty responsibility, but every time we open our mouths or put pen to paper regarding the development of the Marcellus shale, we are taking that responsibility on, for good or ill. Often for both. That's how we symbol-using animals engage with the world. It's messy, but there's a lot of good that comes from the cacophony of voices as long as we can figure out how to make sense of the symbols.

I'm not opposed to the development of natural resources. I cook and heat with gas. Natural gas has the potential to help us with our current energy problems, at least in the short term, and it burns cleaner than other fuels. I'm in favor of people profiting through leases and in local businesses. The problem with the gas industry's development in Tioga County is that most of the information comes from interested parties. Accordingly, the information is shaped in ways that provides a favorable image of the gas industry and of the whole extraction process as safe. Completely. No risks at all. Leave your helmets at home.

This is not surprising, but it is alarming. We have seen what happens in states like West Virginia when extractive industries set the agenda for development. And while our energy needs are real and natural gas provides a fairly clean, short-term alternative, there must be ways to develop the resource that keep community and environmental health in mind. One of the first ways to enact such development is to understand who sets the terms for development and to recognize what they leave out. In Tioga County, the gas industry has done a good job of setting the terms and shaping its information in ways that minimize potential hazards. This tactic was successful partially because the industry encountered little public input.

Living above the Marcellus shale has been a stressful experience because it's difficult to figure out what's going on. I feel like a farmer who needs to feed all his animals at once, their cries growing in frequency and stridency as I rush from grain bin to water trough, trying desperately to catch up. Even though I don't trust the industry, I don't completely trust myself either, because of the messages bombarding me from all sides. I'm standing in the middle of the barnyard with empty buckets, braying, mooing, crowing, cackling, quacking, gobbling, grunting, snorting, oinking, barking, mewing all around me, on the verge of giving up. It's not like I can yell "Quiet!" and gain control of the situation.

Though I've dedicated my life to teaching rhetoric, sometimes I find this cacophony of symbolic acts overwhelming and exhausting and I want to turn off my computer, close all my books, and sit at the fire ring with a bottle of bourbon, staring into the flames. (Okay, I actually do that.) Recognizing that so much of what we understand is based on the way the industry uses symbols unethically, and often seems to be "winning," puts me in a black mood. If we look at the stories of the Gees, the people in Dimock, and elsewhere, we see drilling as a disaster. Reading such stories and facing the implications of them takes a toll. Unless we are from those families, we can't know firsthand the depth of their pain, though we can approximate the experience through the symbolic acts we read about them. Understanding rhetoric means that we have to face unpleasant, even downright depressing stories every time we educate ourselves about what's happening in our places or in the world. Knowing that I can never get outside of language, knowing that it shapes the way I see the world for ill, I find rhetoric frustrating as hell.

But I also find rhetoric hopeful for the same reason: I can never stop the process of trying to understand and arguing for what I want. (Beer and bikes for everyone!) Through rhetoric, I can enter the experiences of others, which make me a better thinker and person. It makes me a better teacher, parent, husband, and member of the community. I can never be satisfied with less than the continual push and pull of a multiplicity of voices arguing for a multiplicity of outcomes. Like a farmer, I can never rest. This is not to suggest that everyone has an equal voice, nor is it to suggest that everyone gets what he wants. But it does mean that the things our symbolic acts show we value can always change. Maybe there's no way to clean up the homes trashed by the gas industry, but there are ways to change what we value to avoid doing it again. That process of enacting change can be slow and frustrating, though Chesapeake's ads claiming "This Is Our Home" show that changes can occur. Likewise, politicians running on the platform of a severance tax suggests they hear the public. Since most of what we understand about the Marcellus shale (and the rest of the world) arises from symbolic knowledge, and symbolic knowledge is not the thing itself, we can create rhetorical acts that provide alternatives and incline people to think differently. Then act.

There are limits to what we can do with language. The gas industry cannot make the fact that it has polluted wells, killed livestock, and destroyed roads go away by ignoring them or calling them "accidents." (I wonder: How many accidents must occur before they are no longer "isolated"?) No matter what the circumstances, the industry always spins things in positive terms. If the message isn't positive, it shuts people up by paying them and making them sign nondisclosure agreements. The signing of nondisclosure agreements or ignoring the issues in the press does not make problems go away, though the industry uses rhetoric to try to do that. Unquestionably, the industry makes it more difficult for us to figure out what's going on by focusing on the positive or the safe or drawing on cultural myths to support its agenda, but it can never completely hide the negative. The asses might be braying loudest, but the other animals need attention as well.

According to scientists, climate change bears down on us at an alarming rate. As the head of the 2013 Intergovernmental Panel on Climate Change reports states, we are at "five minutes to midnight" ("U.N. Researchers" 2013). Many in the gas industry, along with politicians, tout natural gas as a bridge fuel to renewables. This gets us into the ethical dimension of rhetoric. Climate scientists say that we need to stop cranking carbon dioxide into the air *right now*. Yet the gas industry and politicians see the resource as one that burns cleaner than coal and can keep our economy humming as we work toward renewables. It's true that natural gas burns cleaner than coal, but the process of extracting it releases methane. Methane absorbs more heat than carbon dioxide, even though it has a shorter atmospheric life. When I see hundreds of trucks passing my house on Charleston Road pouring diesel smoke into the air or flared wells shining in our windows, I see lots of CO_2 rising into the air. Such physical experiences lead me to believe that the "cleanliness" of gas may be a smoke screen, yet the only way I know that for sure is by reading research on the cleanliness of natural gas represented in symbols (Tollefson 2012, 139–40). If I had to rely on my physical experience, I could guess, but I would not know. That could hurt as much as help us.

—o—

One Sunday morning in late May 2014, I went for a bike ride. Grades were in, though my schedule had not slowed, given that I had become department chair on May 1 and had this book manuscript due. Emails and meetings were frequent; bike rides were not. I coasted down the driveway, turned right on Ore Bed, then right on Scouten Hill Road. I was headed toward the old railroad grade that followed Crooked Creek to Hammond Lake. We had torrential rains Friday, and I wanted to see how high Crooked Creek was and whether the Stephenhouse to Brown Run route had been damaged. Mostly, though, I just wanted to spend some time in the woods away from my computer and phone. Someplace where I couldn't hear any cars or see any words.

I bombed down Scouten Hill Road to Hills Creek Road. A few miles later, I turned right off Hills Creek onto an old railroad grade-turned-gravel road, ducked the south gate, usually open this time of year, and pedaled north toward Hammond Lake. As soon as I rode within sight of the creek, I could see where the waters had jumped the bank. Tall grasses genuflected north, and debris was piled high around the south sides of trees and bushes. Given that the grade here is nearly flat, the creek itself was silent. Pedaling alongside the creek, I saw deep brown water flow around trees and over grasses just a few feet below the railroad grade. I had never seen that much water there, and I marveled at the implacable force of it.

When I noticed the level of the water and the railroad grade slowly converging, I started wondering whether I'd make it to the other end. *Maybe that's why they closed the gate.* One cool thing about bikes is that you can take them under gates, and they are easy to turn around. I kept riding, hoping I could make it to Stephenhouse and the woods.

Soon, trees gave way to fields, and I saw that the shallow pond on the east side of the railroad grade was filled to the brim. A couple of geese swam in the water. For once, I couldn't see any lily pads. I tried to imagine how many gallons of water were spread out over the flat surface, which must be about 300 yards by 100 yards. While I was pulling numbers out of my ass, I rounded a slight bend and saw the road grade disappear under water about 100 yards ahead. Damn. Never saw that before. I slowed and noticed where the pond had broken free of its banks and was pouring over the railroad grade toward Crooked Creek. Given that I was almost at Hammond Lake, the breach made sense.

If one could even call it a breach. The water flooded the road for about 100 yards until the road gained enough elevation to rise from the depths, only to disappear back under water for another 100 yards to the gate marking the north end of the grade. I rode slowly toward the water, wondering what I should do. I'd ridden the railroad grade several times a year since I'd learned of it, usually as fast as possible, racing the other Horses' Asses. I decided the worst that could happen was that I'd drop into an unseen washout and maybe fall. Accelerating, I plunged in.

At first my feet stayed dry, but before long my front hub disappeared and my feet splashed water on every pedal stroke. The water was cold, which made me want to stay upright. Depending on whether the current created ripples, I found I could see through the murky water to the bottom most of the time. I rode through the first section of flooded road without much trouble, so I didn't hesitate before plunging into the second. This section was much like the first, except that I noticed strong currents flowing right to left in front of me not far before the gate. *This could be it*, I thought, and pushed the pedals harder, feet splashing, knowing speed was my friend. I plunged through the ripples, bounced across small ditches cut perpendicular into the road by the current, and cranked into smoother water. I slowed and looked left, digging the idea that I was basically riding in a creek, when splashing pulled my eyes forward. I looked down and saw the back of a carp slicing and splashing through the water, tail whipping, trying to escape my tires, forcing its body forward through the shallows until it hit deeper water and sped off. *Awesome,* I thought. *I've ridden with deer, bears, bobcats, turkeys, foxes, ruffed grouse, bobolinks, red-tail hawks. Now I've ridden with a fish. I love this damn place.*

I pedaled to the gate, hopped off my bike, and lifted it over, thinking about that fish. Then it hit me: Rhetoric is to us what water is to the fish. We're swimming in words, and though we can define rhetoric better than the fish can define water (I hope so, anyway), I'm not confident we *see* it any better. We don't understand the stakes of rhetoric as it functions in our everyday lives as much as we need to. If we did, I'm not sure, environmentally speaking, we'd have ever gotten to where we are. That fish splashed home Burke's point that realizing how much we know is based on nothing but symbols is like peering into an abyss. That fish also thrashed home that the stakes aren't just symbolic. Every decision we make, every position we adopt, every value we argue for affects others, human and more-than-human. The words and images we use to advocate for those decisions, positions, and values point toward some options and hide others. People and places get sacrificed. We have to recognize this and keep talking, writing, and arguing for what we want—a world in which we include as many voices as possible, one giant barnyard.

We're jumping into another kind of abyss if we don't get a grip on this extractive industry thing. Rhetoric helped get us here. And rhetoric will help us make the changes we need to make. How we view land is how we use land. That's driven by rhetoric, and we can change it.

Notes

CHAPTER 1

1. Numbers make up a big part of gas industry rhetoric, and they seem to change weekly, almost daily. These numbers are from Scott Carlson's "Public Colleges Feel the Heat from Gas Boom" (2012). I'm going to throw out a few numbers here and there, but mostly I'm going to ignore them. Numbers don't mean much outside of a context, and I'm more interested in how the context gets shaped. Anyway, the numbers change all the damn time.

2. Ironically of course—women ride and/or drink with us. But the core group is four guys. We call ourselves the Four Horses' Asses of the Apocalypse.

3. Coolidge and his wife own 692 leased acres of dairy farm. They receive "$25 per acre per year," which they use to keep the farm operating. They do not receive royalties because the wells there are not on distribution lines (Przybycien 2013, 12-A).

4. The industry spells "frac" without the "k." I prefer the public's "frack."

5. About six months later, I began to receive monthly Excel spreadsheets from retired MU geography professor Dave Darby that recorded all the industry's environmental violations. Dr. Darby had recorded about ten flowback water violations or spills of various magnitudes that occurred prior to the Wellsboro meeting.

6. Even now, the gas industry sticks to this "not harmful" message in much of its material—material that never shows the possible health risks associated with some of these chemicals. Interested readers should see the Material Safety Data Sheets at the Pennsylvania Department of Environmental Protection's website. In the industry's defense, FracFocus.org provides an (incomplete) database of the chemicals used at well pads.

7. It was illegal to use diesel fuel.

8. Hydrochloric acid is nasty stuff. I've used it to clean concrete.

9. Writing on journalists, media critic Robert McChesney states, "The media do not necessarily tell you what to think, but they tell you what to think about and how to think about it" (2004, 70). Seems applicable here.

10. For example, in logging, tanning, coal mining, and now natural gas.

11. This is one way the natural gas industry fractures communities: it uses language in ways that push people with leases to align themselves with the industry and against neighbors. Kenneth Burke suggests this is "merger by division" (1966, 49–51).

12. New York banned fracking in December 2014.

13. According to the Library of Congress summary, the FRAC Act "(1) repeal[ed] the exemption from restrictions on underground injection of fluids near drinking water sources granted to hydraulic fracturing operations under such Act; and (2) require[d] oil and gas companies to disclose the chemicals used in hydraulic fracturing operations" (http://www.govtrack.us/congress/bills/111/s1215#summary/libraryofcongress). Sponsored by Democratic Senator Bob Casey (PA), the bill died and was referred back to committee.

CHAPTER 2

1. *Citizens United v. Federal Election Commission* is a 2008 Supreme Court case in which the Court decided it was unconstitutional to limit spending by corporations and unions to promote independent political messages about political candidates. Critics argue that the ruling enables corporations to unduly influence election outcomes and that they are treated in the ruling as "persons."

2. To my knowledge, there is no plan to drill in the Lambs Creek Recreational Area.

3. See "'Sense at War with Soul': Arthur's Denial of Wildness Dis-

integrates His Court in Tennyson's *Idylls of the King*," a thesis written in 1999 by James Samuel Guignard Jr. to partially fulfill the master of arts requirement at Western Carolina University. Perhaps no finer thesis has ever been written. Trust me on this.

4. Steingraber's book is about the environmental hazards she documents in Peoria, Illinois, as she struggles with bladder cancer. When I read her book, I saw my visit to Peoria on the truck with Daddy to load slinkys in a new way.

5. Burke talks about maps two paragraphs after the paragraph quoted previously.

CHAPTER 3

1. Feminists, literary critics, and social justice activists have made compelling and important arguments linking the treatment of women to the way we treat the environment. Knowing what I know now, I could have done more with these ideas in my master's thesis.

2. As Jenny Edbauer puts it, "[the] rhetorical situation is better conceptualized as a mixture of processes and encounters" (2005, 13).

3. Burke published *The Rhetoric of Motives* in 1950, which means he envisioned a barnyard with multiple species of animals, all braying, honking, mooing, baaing, clucking, crowing, barking, mewing, oinking, chirping, and cursing. He was not talking about confined animal feeding operations, where thousands of cows or pigs all speak in one (loud) voice.

4. Between 2000 and 2009, *The New York Times* database showed thirty-five articles for the phrase "Marcellus Shale"; from 2010 until early 2012, it showed seventy-three records. For another 1,521 US newspapers (excluding the *Times*), NewsBank showed 1 hit for "Marcellus shale" in 2007; 216 hits in 2008; 403 hits in 2009; 2,014 hits in 2010; and 2,954 hits in 2011. In contrast, the ABI/INFORM Trade and Industry database showed 12 hits for "Marcellus shale" in 2006; 85 hits in 2007; 1,085 hits in 2008; 1,200 hits in 2009; 2,058 hits in 2010; and 2,311 hits in 2011. It's worth noting that *The New York Times* and NewsBank listed articles

that supported and questioned the industry, which means the industry has always had the louder voice in the public sphere.

5. Dimock has been written about exhaustively. For more accounts, see Legere (2009) and Wilbur (2009).

6. Tom Wilbur covered the natural gas industry for the *Press & Sun-Bulletin* for several years, eventually turning his reporting into a book called *Under the Surface: Fracking, Fortunes, and the Fate of the Marcellus Shale*. He maintains a blog called *Shale Gas Review* at http://tomwilber.blogspot.com/.

7. Around six months after I read Legere and Wilbur's reporting, the *Wellsboro Gazette* began printing similar stories.

8. Granted, an accent is not a message in the sense we've been looking at, but an accent is a part of any message and, depending on audience and purpose, can make persuading someone to think a particular way or to take a particular action easier or more difficult. Much to my chagrin, I've lost much of my accent. Even though I swore it wouldn't, graduate school beat it out of me.

9. Check us out at pipelineroad7.wordpress.com.

10. There are likely many reasons for this. Two that come to mind are out-of-state workers don't have time to learn original names and safety vehicles need detail about pipeline sections. However, there's no denying the abstracting dimension of the signs.

11. Tioga County has a less than stellar record with extractive industries. For example, acid mine drainage from coal mining has essentially killed the Tioga River, which runs right through Mansfield.

12. For a more detailed discussion, see Lakoff and Johnson (1981).

13. Employment numbers grew locally during 2009 and 2010 alongside the development of the gas resource. According to the Bureau of Labor Statistics, Tioga County had one of the lowest rates of unemployment in Pennsylvania during that time.

14. We have to watch who funds university research these days. Researchers have found that studies funded by interested parties show a

higher rate of reaching conclusions agreeable to the funder than studies funded by disinterested parties.

15. Penn State faculty also produced quality, disinterested research about the effects of gas drilling on rural counties, but the "Emerging Giant" research was what reached me.

CHAPTER 4

1. The local paper is the *Wellsboro Gazette*, based in Wellsboro, Pennsylvania, though a different edition called the *Mansfield Gazette* is printed for Mansfield 12 miles away. I bought the Mansfield edition until I moved to the country. Same content in both; different layouts of the first page.

2. At the time, this brought East's holdings up to 253,328.23 leased acres.

3. East even sponsored the local mountain bike race a few times.

4. In the report, I'm the audience member she mentions who asked the question about a severance tax.

5. As Shell's buyout of East was occurring, BP was trying to plug that leaking well in the Gulf. Reading about their shenanigans and watching news footage of the well spewing oil did not ease my mind either.

6. I'm counting pickups, dump trucks, water trucks, sand trucks, and flatbeds loaded with drilling equipment. I'm not counting trucks that did not clearly work for the industry.

7. For a lesson in how BP tried to cover up its mess in the Gulf, see Gessner (2012).

8. In 2011 the university fast-tracked two programs through the curricular process designed to benefit the industry, a bachelor of science in safety management and an associate of applied science in natural gas production and services.

9. In questioning Howarth's activism, both organizations conveniently overlooked the fact that they themselves are funded by the industry.

10. In small print, the ad stated, "Ms. Brockovich appears as a paid, non-lawyer endorser." I'm not sure how to take that.

11. A wind trainer is a modern torture device whereby you convert your bicycle into a stationary bike by attaching a frame with a small, fluid-filled aluminum drum to the rear tire. The drum provides resistance. They work well, but they are boring. Hence meeting at the shop.

12. Pacelining refers to cyclists riding in a tight, single-file formation and taking advantage of the draft. Cyclists rotate off the front of the line regularly and fall into line at the end, giving them a chance to catch their breath in the slipstream formed by the line. Because of the physics of the paceline, a group of cyclists working together is faster than a single cyclist, and it is an absolute joy to be a part of.

13. A great cycling term for a situation in which riders try to make other riders suffer by sprinting, attacking the hills, or pushing the speed of the paceline.

CHAPTER 5

1. This strategy works the same way in reverse: a scary image will override a positive message.

2. This doesn't mean such images don't ring true. There's no denying Manifest Destiny. But such images and the way they are used tell only part of the story.

3. One term I've found useful for thinking about images as rhetoric comes from Kevin Michael DeLuca's (1999) *Image Politics*. Drawing on Michael Calvin McGee's work, DeLuca uses the term "ideograph" to describe "an ordinary-language term found in political discourse. It is a high-order abstraction representing collective commitment to a particular but equivocal and ill-defined normative goal. It warrants the use of power, excuses behavior and belief which might otherwise be perceived as eccentric or antisocial, and guides behavior and belief into channels easily recognizable by a community as acceptable and laudable" (36). Whew. DeLu-

ca's usefulness comes from the way he uses this framework to understand the historical and contingent nature of images and the accompanying sloppiness. In *Image Politics*, he focuses his analysis on ideographs from environmental movements, though his ideas help me understand gas industry rhetoric.

4. Unlike me, who may have little to show except comments on students' papers or a shitty draft of a book chapter. Sometimes I miss the straightforwardness of framing a house.

5. Weber (1905/1992) provides a good place to start when thinking about how our modern infatuation with making money for the sake of making money seems almost religious.

6. The public seems to buy the idea that Jesus was a carpenter, but I've found little evidence to support it. It makes a great bumper sticker though.

7. I confess the images tug at me too.

8. Few women work on the rigs, though I suspect this "tough" frame appeals to some. "Drilling" is a masculine world (and rife with metaphor.)

9. "RENEWAL" and "PROSPERITY" could easily apply to the gas industry's hopes for America as well.

10. Actually, most came from Texas, Utah, Wyoming, Oklahoma, and Louisiana.

11. A number of books talk about the problems with big agribusiness farms, the opposite of farms we see around here. I like Eric Schlosser's *Fast Food Nation* (Boston: Houghton Mifflin, 2001) and Michael Pollan's *The Botany of Desire* (New York: Random House, 2001).

12. Lilace says this is one of her motivations for moving, but she didn't want to tell me at the time because I'd say I *wasn't* working too much. She's right.

13. See "Focusing Public Attention—And Staying with a Story Relentlessly" on ProPublica's website (http://www.propublica.org/about/focusing-public-attention-and-staying-with-a-story-relentlessly). An independent, nonprofit news organization, ProPublica has provided insightful

reporting on the gas industry. The article accompanying the photo tells the story of ProPublica's doggedness in following the fracking story since early 2008, when many other journalists were not. The article sings the praises of reporter Abrahm Lustgarten and includes links to ten articles about the natural gas industry. ProPublica has been a go-to source for me since I learned of its reporting in 2008.

14. For some reason, many people in the United States think that most of our oil comes from the Middle East. This is not the case. We import most of our oil from Canada and Latin America. We import about the same amount from Africa as we do the Middle East. See Lisa Margonelli's (2007) *Oil on the Brain: Adventures from the Pump to the Pipeline*.

15. The industry still claims this, though it is talking about the act of fracking specifically, whereas the public defines the whole drilling process as "fracking." For something so "safe," I sure have seen a lot of damage.

16. The financial situation at my university has been another source of confusion.

CHAPTER 7

1. Read more about Stop the Frack Attack at http://www.stopthe frackattack.org/.

2. Much to my chagrin, I found little news coverage of the rally, which begs the question of whether the rally had any sort of meaningful impact. That said, I think it mattered that all those people came together if for no other reason than it added to the paper-thin lines of our particular lives. Words may create most of what we know, but the memory of 5,000 like-minded people marching in the heat to make a point can be energizing.

3. Paul noted that the Environmental Protection Agency has not stated any limits for human exposure to strontium. I would like it to set a level. Now.

4. Often a word associated with "bullshit."

References

Abbey, Edward. *Desert Solitaire: A Season in the Wilderness.* New York: Simon & Schuster, 1990. (Originally published 1968)

Adelbeck, Hannah. "The Risks of Marcellus Shale Drilling Are Worth the Potential Gains, Says PSU Prof." *Voices of Central Pennsylvania,* June 10, 2010. http://voicesweb.org

Burke, Kenneth. *A Grammar of Motives.* New York: Prentice-Hall, 1945.
———. *A Rhetoric of Motives.* New York: Prentice-Hall, 1950.
———. *Language as Symbolic Action: Essays on Life, Literature, and Method.* Berkeley: University of California Press, 1966.

Carlson, Scott. "Colleges Atop Gas-Rich Shale Weigh Offers from Drillers." *The Chronicle of Higher Education* 56.39 (2010): A1, A13.
———. "Public Colleges Feel the Heat from Gas Boom." *The Chronicle of Higher Education,* July 16, 2012. http://chronicle.com

Clarke, Cheryl R. "Tioga County Family Struggles with Methane in Its Well Water." *Williamsport Sun-Gazette,* July 2, 2011. http://www.sungazette.com
———. "Speaker: Study of Water Wells near Gas Drilling Is Encouraging." *Williamsport Sun-Gazette,* December 19, 2013. http://www.sungazette.com

Considine, Timothy, Robert Watson, Rebecca Entler, and Jeffrey Sparks. "An Emerging Giant: Prospects and Economic Impacts of Developing the Marcellus Shale Natural Gas Play." Marcellus Shale Coalition, August 5, 2009. http://marcelluscoalition.org/wp-content/uploads/2010/05/EconomicImpactsofDevelopingMarcellus.pdf

Cooper, Marilyn. "The Ecology of Writing." *College English* 48 (1986): 364–75.

DeLuca, Kevin Michael. *Image Politics: The New Rhetoric of Environmental Activism.* New York: Routledge, 1999.

Doyle, Leonard. "Shell Execs Accused of 'Collaboration' over Hanging of Nigerian Activist Ken Saro-Wiwa." *The Telegraph,* May 31, 2009. http://www.telegraph.co.uk

"East Resources Supports Tioga County 4-H with $50,000." *Wellsboro Gazette,* March 3, 2010: 1-A.

Edbauer, Jenny. "Unframing Models of Public Distribution: From Rhetorical Situation to Rhetorical Ecologies." *Rhetoric Society Quarterly* 35.4 (2005): 5–24.

Engelder, Terry, and Gary G. Lash. "Marcellus Shale Play's Vast Resource Potential Creating a Stir in Appalachia." *The American Oil and Gas Reporter,* May 2008. http://www.marcellus.psu.edu/resources/PDFs/EngelderLash080GRept.pdf

"Five Things to Know about the Cornell Shale Study (Courtesy of Energy in Depth)." Marcellus Shale Coalition, April 13, 2011. http://energyindepth.org

Gessner, David. *The Tarball Chronicles: A Journey Beyond the Oiled Pelican and Into the Heart of the Gulf Oil Spill.* Minneapolis: Milkweed Editions, 2012.

Goleman, Daniel. *Ecological Intelligence: The Hidden Impacts of What We Buy.* New York: Broadway Books, 2009.

Heinberg, Richard. *Snake Oil: How Fracking's False Promise of Plenty Imperils Our Future.* Santa Rosa, CA: Post Carbon Institute, 2013.

Howarth, Robert W., Renee Santoro, and Anthony Ingraffea. "Methane and the Greenhouse-Gas Footprint of Natural Gas from Shale Formations: A Letter." *Climatic Change* 106 (2011): 679–90.

Ingraffea, Anthony. "Fluid Migration Mechanisms Due to Faulty Well Design and/or Construction: An Overview and Recent Experiences in the Pennsylvania Marcellus Play." Physicians, Scientists, and Engineers for Healthy Energy, January 2013. http://psehealthyenergy.org/data/PSE__Cement_Failure_Causes_and_Rate_Analaysis_Jan_2013_Ingraffea1.pdf

Jiang, Mohan, W. Michael Griffin, Chris Hendrickson, Paulina Jaramillo,

Jeanne VanBriesen, and Aranya Venkates. "Lifecycle Greenhouse Gas Emissions of Marcellus Shale Gas." *Environmental Research Letters* 6 (2011): 1–9.

Kennedy, Natalie. "Marcellus Committee Addresses 125 People at Wellsboro Meeting." *Wellsboro Gazette,* June 10, 2009: 1-A.

———. "New Study Tracks Marcellus Shale Drilling Violations." *Mansfield Gazette*, August 4, 2010a: 1-A.

———. "University Plans to Cut Programs, Staff." *Mansfield Gazette,* May 26, 2010b: 1-A.

Lakoff, George, and Mark Johnson. *Metaphors We Live By*. Chicago: University of Chicago Press, 1981.

Legere, Laura. "Cabot Must Ensure Water Supply." *The Times-Tribune,* November 5, 2009: A1.

Lustgarten, Abrahm. "Officials in Three States Pin Water Woes on Gas Drilling." ProPublica, 2009. www.propublica.org

"Marcellus Shale—Appalachian Basin Natural Gas Play." Geology.com, n.d. http://geology.com/articles/marcellus-shale.shtml

"Marcellus Shale Committee Issues Statement on Severance Tax." Press release. Marcellus Shale Coalition, February 4, 2009.

Margonelli, Lisa. *Oil on the Brain: Adventures from the Pump to the Pipeline*. New York: Doubleday, 2007.

Marx, Leo. *The Machine in the Garden: Technology and the Pastoral Ideal in America*. London: Oxford University Press, 1964.

McChesney, Robert. *The Problem of the Media: U.S. Communication Politics in the Twenty-First Century*. New York: Monthly Review Press, 2004.

Nelson, Richard. *The Island Within*. New York: Vintage, 1995.

———. *Heart and Blood: Living with Deer in America*. New York: Vintage, 1997.

"Opportunity." Marcellus Shale Coalition, 2012. http://marcelluscoalition.org

"PA's Oil, Gas Industry Opposes Fracture Stimulation Reporting Bill in Congress." Press release. Marcellus Shale Coalition, July 10, 2009.

Powers, Bill. *Cold, Hungry and in the Dark*. Gabriola, BC: New Society, 2013.

Przybycien, Jason. "County Inks East Leases." *Wellsboro Gazette,* February 3, 2010a: 1-A.

———. "Drilling into the Shale Business: Meet East Resources, Inc." *Mansfield Gazette,* February 3, 2010b: 14.

———. "State Watches Cows after Frack Spill." *Wellsboro Gazette,* June 30, 2010c: 1-A.

———. "Who Has a Gas Lease?" *Wellsboro Gazette,* August 28, 2013: 1-A, 12-A.

Rhoads, Stephen W. "Marcellus Shale Tax Won't Solve Budget Woes." *Harrisburg Patriot-News,* June 15, 2009.

Rubinkam, Michael. "Gas CEO Takes on Protesters." *Times Leader,* September 8, 2011: 4A.

Scheese, Don. *Nature Writing: The Pastoral Impulse in America*. 1995. New York: Routledge, 2002.

"$haleionaires: Shale Gas Drilling: Pros and Cons." *60 Minutes*. Host Lesley Stahl. Prod. Shachar Bar-On and Meghan Frank. CBS, November 14, 2010.

"Shell Will Buy East Resources." *Mansfield Gazette,* June 2, 2010: 1-A.

Siwy, Bruce. "Corbett Touts Johnstown Manufacturing Plant." *Daily American,* December 22, 2011. http://www.dailyamerican.com

Snyder, Gary. *The Practice of the Wild*. Berkeley, CA: North Point Press, 1990.

"The Marcellus Shale: Energy to Fuel our Future." Marcellus Shale Coalition, 2012. http://marcelluscoalition.org/

Tollefson, Jeff. "Air Sampling Reveals High Emissions from Gas Fields." *Nature* 482.7384 (2012): 139–40.

Turner, Frederick Jackson. *The Frontier in American History*. New York: Henry Holt, 1921.

Tuan, Yi-Fu. *Space and Place: The Perspective of Experience*. Minneapolis: University of Minnesota Press, 1977.

Ulrich, John. "Report on the Department Meeting on Retrenchment." November 13, 2011.

"U.N. Researchers: Global Warming Clock is at 'Five Minutes to Midnight.'" *RawStory.com*, September 2, 2013. http://www.rawstory.com

Watson, Robert W. "Sunday Forum: The Bottom Line on Marcellus Shale." *Pittsburgh Post-Gazette,* July 19, 2009.

Warner, Michael. *Publics and Counterpublics.* New York: Zone Books, 2002.

Weber, Max. *The Protestant Ethic and the Spirit of Capitalism.* Translated by Talcott Parsons. New York: Routledge, 1992. (Originally published 1905)

Welch, Nancy. *Living Room: Teaching Public Writing in a Privatized World.* Portsmouth, NH: Boynton/Cook, 2008.

"What Is Residual Waste Fact Sheet." Harrisburg: Pennsylvania Department of Environmental Protection, 2015. http://www.portal.state.pa.us/portal/server.pt?open=514&objID=589699&mode=2

Wilbur, Tom. "State Files Outline Drilling Accidents." *Press & Sun-Bulletin*, November 9, 2009: 1A, 5A.

Wilde, Oscar. *The Decay of Lying: An Observation.* London: Penguin, 1995. (Originally published 1889)

Zuckerman, Gregory. *The Frackers: The Outrageous Inside Story of the New Billionaire Wildcatters.* New York: Portfolio, 2013.

Index